THE

IMPERFECT

PANACEA:

AMERICAN FAITH IN EDUCATION

Consulting Editor: PAUL NASH, *Boston University*

HENRY J. PERKINSON

New York University

THE IMPERFECT PANACEA:

AMERICAN FAITH IN EDUCATION, 1865–1976

Second Edition

RANDOM HOUSE New York

Second Edition

987654

Copyright © 1968, 1977 by Henry J. Perkinson
All rights reserved under International and Pan-American Copyright Conventions. No part of this book may be reproduced in any form or by any means, electronic or mechanical, including photocopying, without permission in writing from the publisher. All inquiries should be addressed to Random House, Inc., 201 East 50th Street, New York, N.Y. 10022. Published in the United States by Random House, Inc., and simultaneously in Canada by Random House of Canada Limited, Toronto.

Library of Congress Cataloging in Publication Data

Perkinson, Henry J
  The imperfect panacea.

  "Bibliographical note": p.
  1. Education—United States—History.   2. Education—Philosophy.   I. Title.
LA209.P422   1977   370'.973   76-45395
ISBN 0-394-31216-3

Manufactured in the United States of America

For Audrey

"Just see wherever we peer into the first tiny springs of the national life, how this true panacea for all the ills of the body politic bubbles forth—education, education, education."

ANDREW CARNEGIE

"The answer for all our national problems comes down to one single word: education."

LYNDON B. JOHNSON

PREFACE TO THE SECOND EDITION

What are schools for? Can schools solve racial problems? provide equal economic opportunity for all? reconstruct our cities? insure political greatness? In this book I try to show that American schools have tried to do all these things, but failed. In this edition I have added an epilogue that relates the events of the last ten years to my thesis, enlarging it to argue that schooling—as we presently construe it—can neither cure our social ills nor help people escape from them.

History records the unanticipated consequences of past human actions, so that we may learn from our mistakes. But history cannot tell us what we should do. It is we, not history, who must decide what schools are for.

Henry J. Perkinsor

PREFACE TO THE FIRST EDITION

One day while she was typing the manuscript for this book, my secretary looked up and asked me, "If the schools can't solve these problems, then who can?" This question rests on what I consider to be two basic assumptions of most Americans: first, that all social problems are solvable; second, that the schools are the panacea for all social problems. I continue to hope that the first assumption is warranted, but I have begun to have serious doubts about the second, and that is why I have written this book and given it the title I have.

Although the book spans the years 1865–1965, I have focused on the period between the Civil War and the First World War, because this is, I think, the formative era in American education. I am indebted to the work of those who have made intensive examinations of this era, especially Richard Hofstadter, Eric Goldman, C. Vann Woodward, Arthur M. Schlesinger, Sidney Fine, Harold Faulkner, Lawrence A. Cremin, Merle Curti, and Edward Krug. I have also been influenced and greatly helped by the published work of Rush Welter, who was the first to point out the centrality of education in the history of the American people. I do not think that one can fully understand American history without some appreciation of the centrality of education. Here I concentrate primarily on formal education, the schools, because my contention is that the American faith in the power of education has led all of us to make unwarranted, unrealistic, and harmful demands upon it.

Henry J. Perkinson

CONTENTS

THE
IMPERFECT
PANACEA:
AMERICAN FAITH IN EDUCATION

ONE || AMERICANS AND THEIR SCHOOLS

I

From the beginning Americans depended on their schools. Alone in the savage wilderness of their new settlements, the earliest colonists had to rely upon schools and schoolteachers far more than they did in Europe. Forced to spend their days securing the basic necessities of life, these pioneer parents had little time to care for their children. Moreover, since their New World lacked the agencies of civilization commonplace in the mother country, parents in the New World feared that their children, if untended, might degenerate into savagery—not an unlikely fate in this strange, wild, and dangerous land.

In the colony of Massachusetts this fear resulted in the 1642 compulsory education law, which made parents legally responsible for the education of their children. The problem, of course, lay not with parents, who, for the most part, wanted to educate their children, but in finding the time and energy to care for them. The colony realized that it needed schools and schoolmasters, and in 1647 Massachusetts adopted a law that required each town to provide them. Thus it happened that the first compulsory education laws of modern times appeared in the least civilized part of the Western world and, in fact, were a product of that very lack of civilization.

Other New England colonies copied the Massachusetts compulsory education laws, and in the Middle Atlantic colonies the settlers similarly relied heavily on schools and schoolmasters. The Quakers, a year after their arrival in Pennsylvania in 1682, asked Enoch Flower to become a schoolmaster in Philadelphia and in the same year adopted a compulsory education law.

The Dutch in New Netherlands never had any laws or statutes concerning compulsory education, but they did establish a number of schools to care for their children. The absence of laws is less surprising than the existence of schools since the colony was actually not much more than a hunting and trapping preserve, attracting single men in search of fortune and adventure. A few families did come to settle, and these parents also turned to schools and schoolmasters to do what they found impossible to do alone. When the British acquired this colony in the late seventeenth century, much of the wilderness had been tamed. Consequently, the English families who came to New York had little fear for their children and, thus, no great concern for schools or schoolmasters. This helps to explain the colony's frequently noted "policy of indifference toward educational legislation." Yet this indifference to educational legislation should not be taken as an indifference to schools and schooling. The New Yorkers did not have to look to the schools to preserve civilization; civilization was secure. Instead they looked to the schools to perform a different yet no less vital function: to prepare children for the unexpected.

II

Throughout its early history America suffered from a short supply of labor. In the South this led to the introduction of Negro slaves. In the rest of the country it led to a decline in the system of apprenticeship. While in Europe future physicians, lawyers, merchants, bankers, artisans, and craftsmen of all kinds received their training through apprenticeship, in the New World the short supply of labor prevented the American from becoming a specialist. Rather than apprenticing himself to one master to learn one skill well, the colonial American had to learn to perform many different tasks. He frequently had to provide his own clothing and shelter, clear the land and plant the crops, tend his animals and care for his children, and nurse the sick and settle disputes. He had to be a jack-of-all-trades; he could not afford to be a specialist. To get along, the American had to be, in Daniel Boorstin's words, "an undifferentiated man." *

Since Europe had no labor shortage, it could continue to train children for specific jobs, jobs suited to their social status. In Europe each child expected to enter a specific occupation, which could usually be predicted with a fair amount of accuracy since the social position

* Complete references for quoted material found throughout the text are contained in the Bibliographic Note (pp. 237–251), arranged according to chapter.

of his family (and frequently his position in the family —the eldest son, for example, inherited the father's estate) inevitably determined career opportunities.

But in America a child's future was indeterminate. Even in the cities that were well established by the eighteenth century, the expanding economy and the shifting population combined to produce unlimited and unexpected opportunities for all. The problem, then, was to prepare for the unexpected. Yet how could this be done? In an unfamiliar, unknown land there was no one to learn from.

On the frontier farm, or in the forests, one learned from one's own experience. There were no other guides. But in the settled cities on the Eastern seaboard the case was different, since one found trade and commerce carried on in more or less traditional ways. There, the young American preparing for the future never knew what business, calling, or profession he might enter. It was to help solve this problem of urban youth that Benjamin Franklin set forth, in his "Idea of the English School, Sketch'd Out for the Consideration of the Trustees of the Philadelphia Academy," a proposal for a school in Philadelphia, from which youth "will come out . . . fitted for learning *any* Business, calling, or Profession." This proposal to use the school to prepare youths for the unexpected was not a novel one. Throughout the late seventeenth and the eighteenth centuries private "adventure" schools had sprung up in all of the Eastern towns and cities. These schools usually consisted of one teacher, who provided instruction in a great number of "modern subjects": commercial subjects, including arithmetic, accounting, bookkeeping, penmanship, letter writing; pure and applied mathematics, including engineering, surveying, navigation; modern foreign languages,

Spanish, French, Portuguese; as well as geography and history.

Franklin's contribution lay in his attempt to establish a permanent school, an academy, which would take the "adventure" out of such schooling. With the academy, he hoped to institutionalize and guarantee the continuation of the kind of instruction heretofore dependent upon the immobility and longevity of the private teachers. Actually the academy, after a few years, strayed from Franklin's original purpose, becoming primarily a Latin grammar school. Franklin then severed his connections with it, asserting that it "was no longer concerned with education for such a country as ours."

Although his own academy was a sore disappointment, others took up Franklin's idea for a permanent school where youths could be prepared for the unexpected. By the end of the century academies had been set up in all parts of the country, offering both modern and traditional subjects. Yet even as the academy idea triumphed, other educational developments took center stage. Once they had gained their independence from Britain, the Americans looked to the schools and the schoolmasters to perform a new function: a political function.

III

As soon as the War for Independence ended, Americans began to talk about the vital relationship between education and government. In the 1790's the American Philosophical Society sponsored a contest to select the best essay on a "system of Liberal Education and Literary Instruction adapted to the genius of government. . . ." Most accepted the claim that in a republic the chief end of education is to promote intelligent citizenship. This followed logically from the American negative conception of government, a conception embodied succinctly in the statement, "that government is best that governs least." Fearful of governmental tyranny the Americans had set up a national government that could be restrained and held in check. To do this they had adopted a variety of institutional devices: a Bill of Rights; a written Constitution that enumerated specific powers; a separation of the three branches of government, with each one having the power to veto, or check, the others; and regular, frequent elections, so that the citizens could peacefully get rid of undesirables in public office. But the proper working of all these institutional devices depended upon an enlightened citizenry, an educated citizenry. No one saw this more clearly than Thomas Jefferson. In a letter to George Washington in 1786 he wrote: "It is an axiom of my mind that our liberty can never be safe but in the hands of the people themselves, and that too of the people with a certain degree of instruction."

Jefferson went on to say that he thought this "is the business of the state to effect, and on a general plan." A few years earlier he had submitted to the Virginia legislature just such a general plan for a statewide system of schools, the famous "Bill for the More General Diffusion of Knowledge." Here we find clearly articulated the new political function expected of the schools: "experience has shown," he wrote, "that even under the best forms [of government], those entrusted with power have, in time, and by slow operations, perverted it into tyranny and it is believed that the most effective means of preventing this would be to illuminate, as far as practicable, the minds of the people at large."

During this early national period each state government, in one way or another, did encourage the setting up of schools. Usually this took the form of financial help—anything from the allotment of special tax revenues to state lotteries. Sometimes the state donated grants of land for schools. Most states created a permanent fund to provide school grants.

Encouragement for the creation of schools came from the national government as well. The famous Northwest Ordinance of 1787 required each township in the Northwest Territory to set aside a mile square section of land for educational purposes. This ordinance captured perfectly the sentiment of most Americans when it declared: "Religion, morality, and knowledge being necessary to good government and the happiness of mankind, schools and the means of education should forever be encouraged."

The same Northwest Ordinance provided that each state in the territory must set aside not more than two townships "for the purposes of a seminary of learning." This concern with higher education also had its roots in the political theory of the new nation. In contrast to the political practices of Europe where governmental power was in the hands of a hereditary aristocracy, the Founding Fathers proclaimed that theirs was a free society, an open society, where positions of power were accessible to all men. They fondly hoped that this openness of their society would allow men of talent to rise to positions of leadership, regardless of their ancestry or their economic status. Rejecting the artificial aristocracies of the Old World, the Americans looked for, as Jefferson put it, "a national aristocracy of talent."

The identification, cultivation, and preparation of these men of talent became the task of the schools. The schools were expected to produce future leaders. Jefferson's plan for the state of Virginia clearly embodied this function of selecting and training leaders. His proposed hierarchical educational system would, he declared, rake the best geniuses "from the rubbish."

Few, other than Jefferson, saw the necessity for an entire system of education, but most did see the need for institutions of higher learning to perform this political function of producing leaders. During this early national period a number of prominent statesmen—including George Washington, James Madison, and John Quincy Adams—publicly proposed the establishment of a national university. Religion and political difficulties prevented its inception. However, throughout the country colleges and universities sprang up. Some were private, usually religious, institutions; others were public or state colleges. By 1799 America had 25 institutions of higher learning. Only twenty-five years earlier there had been but 9. By 1820 the number of colleges had increased to 50.

IV

By the 1820's a new political theory had emerged in America. In opposition to the beliefs of the Founding Fathers, these new democrats, usually called Jacksonian democrats, preached a theory of popular sovereignty. They rejected all elites, all aristocracies —natural or not—in favor of rule by the people themselves.

The rise of Jacksonian democracy brought about a transformation in the political function of the schools. First of all, the Jacksonian democrats opposed colleges and universities, regarding them as the "seedbed of aristocracies," or more colloquially, "places for dudes."

Actually, the number of colleges continued to climb during the Age of the Common Man, reaching 182 by 1860. This proliferation of institutions of higher learning is usually credited to the intensification of religious rivalry and hometown "boosterism." Here the Americans used schools of higher learning as symbols of prestige. The emptiness of this function is best illustrated by the fact that more than 80 percent of the colleges founded during this period failed and disappeared. Religious and hometown pride had created the colleges, but they needed students to stay in business, and these were hard to find. Once the ascendancy of Jacksonian democracy had undermined the political function of the colleges, there was little need for Americans to attend college. This anomalous situation of abundant numbers of colleges with few students in attendance lasted until after the Civil War when the American colleges acquired a new function and regained relevance to American life.

Although Jacksonian democracy had a deleterious impact on the development of higher education, it hastened the development of the "American common school." Actually, as Rush Welter shows in *Popular Education and Democratic Thought in America,* the conception of an equal, free education for all was implicit in the earlier political theory of the Founding Fathers. Their desire for an open society ruled by an aristocracy of talent required universal schooling so that those of ability could be selected and sent on to the higher levels to continue their education.

The Jacksonian democrats, while they agreed with the need for universal schooling, saw the school as an equalizer rather than a selector. That is, for them the school had the task of eliminating all privilege and destroying all elites by giving to all men the same good common education. The Jacksonian democrats did not look upon the schools as a device for sorting the gems from the rubbish, but as a social institution that might help to make all men equal. Horace Eaton, first State Superintendent of Schools in Vermont, expressed this clearly in his first report: "Let every child in the land enjoy the advantages of a competent education at his outset in life—and it will do more to secure a general equality of condition than any guarantee of equal rights and privileges which constitution or laws can give." He referred to the common schools as "an equalizing power —a levelling engine." By the 1850's almost every Northern state had provided common schools, and as Welter notes, "there was no turning back."

For over 200 years the Americans had looked to their schools and schoolmasters to solve their social, economic, and political problems. From the beginnings the schools had been viewed as the panacea—first to preserve civilization, then to prepare for the unexpected, and finally to guarantee good government. After the Civil War the Americans faced a host of new problems and as before they turned to their schools.

TWO ‖ RACIAL INEQUALITY
AND THE SCHOOLS

I

It was only six months after Appomattox when Francis Wayland, the president of Brown
University, told the National Teachers Association that
the root of the recent deluge of blood lay "in the fact of
a diffused and universal education in the North and a
very limited education of the South." "The Civil War,"
he explained, "had been a war of education and patriot-
ism against ignorance and barbarism." President Wayland was not alone in viewing the recent holocaust in
educational terms. Many Northerners shared his belief
that the educational backwardness of the South had precipitated the war. This conviction stemmed not from
some idle speculation about the causes of the Civil War,
but from a serious concern with the problem of victory:

the restoration of the Union. If the War Between the States was looked at in educational terms, then reunion became possible. Education would restore the Union. Education must be diffused throughout the South; black and white alike must be educated. Not to educate them was to court another war.

President Wayland was sounding a clarion call in Chicago when he asked, "Can we not as educators go boldly into Southern states and teach the truth and the whole truth?" Actually, hordes of Yankee teachers had already invaded the South. President Wayland and the National Teachers Association were too late to be bell-wethers. The descent had begun while the war was still going on, with teachers pressing hard on the heels of the soldiers.

As early as 1862, the New England Freedmen's Aid Society sent 72 teachers to Port Royal, Virginia. Another organization, the American Missionary Society, founded as an abolitionist society in 1846, remained active during the war by supplying teachers who literally "followed the army." By 1866 this society had 353 teachers in the field. All together, there were at least seventy-nine different philanthropic associations concerned with sending teachers to the South. Some of these societies were strictly denominational, like the Freedmen's Aid Society of the Methodist Episcopal Church, which established fifty-nine schools, sent out 124 teachers, and expended over $60,000 during the first two years of its work. Some of these philanthropic associations were large and impressive, like the American Union Commission with offices in New York, Boston, Philadelphia, Baltimore, and Chicago. Others were small local associations that were short-lived. The great variety and number of different associations sending teachers into the South make it impossible to determine just how many Northern teachers actually went into the South during this period.

The educational work of these various philanthropic associations was frequently carried out in cooperation with the Freedmen's Bureau. Established in 1865 as the Bureau of Refugees, Freedmen, and Abandoned Lands, this federal agency was responsible for the relief of freedmen through medical and hospital service and supplies, through the supervision of labor contracts, through the control of all confiscated or abandoned lands, and, finally, through the establishment of schools. It was this last function of the bureau that was the special concern of its head, General O. O. Howard, who by his own admission devoted more attention to education than to any other branch of his work. The bureau, operating with funds obtained by the sale of confiscated Confederate property, usually set up the schools while the philanthropic associations supplied the teachers. In many instances the bureau supplied its own teachers; frequently these teachers were newly freed Negroes, some of whom, unfortunately, were barely able to read and write.

The Freedmen's Bureau did keep records for the teachers under its jurisdiction. According to these records it had 972 teachers in the field in January 1867. By the following year, the number had increased to 2,948 teachers. The peak period for the bureau was July 1869, when a total of 9,503 white and Negro teachers were reported in the field.

What was the Southern reaction to this invasion of Yankee schoolteachers bent upon the educational reconstruction of the South? It does not take much imagination to understand that many Southerners saw this educational reconstruction as an attempt to add insult and humiliation to the military defeat. The fact that most of these Northern teachers were women was an additional affront to the Southerner's pride. Nor did the demeanor of the Yankee teachers help matters since, for the most part, they regarded the Southerners as sinners whom they had come to redeem with "the truth, the whole truth." The white Southerner, therefore, came to regard these Yankee schoolmarms with coolness, perhaps with disdain, and even with contempt. The Southern whites were not concerned with reconstructing themselves, at least not in the way the Northerners meant. The South, after all, had fought for the right to secede from the Union, the right to preserve its way of life. The South had lost, and one could hardly expect the defeated to have the same concerns as the victor. After losing the war, the South had its own concern: the freed slave.

What did freedom mean? One thing was certain: it meant that the Negro was no longer the property of the white man. But did it mean that now the Negro was to be accepted as a man, a black man, equal to the white man? If this is what freedom meant, then the white Southerner saw himself divested of both his property *and* his status. But more than status was involved in the white Southerner's refusal to associate with former slaves as equals. If the Negroes were treated as equal then they might, in many instances, in many areas, dominate the white man. And perhaps even greater than fear of black domination was the fear of Negro retaliation for former injustices. The white man was afraid—afraid for his property, his culture, his very life. The Southerner felt that the Negro must be constrained, must be dominated, must be segregated. To accomplish these ends, the defeated South now began passing laws that imposed the yoke of servility upon the supposedly freed slaves. During the years 1865 and 1866 every Confederate state except

Tennessee passed Black Codes limiting the freedman's life with varying degrees of severity. The Negro's right to hold property was restrained, as well as his right to sue and be sued, and to have legal marriages and off-spring. Negroes could appear as witness only in cases where one or both parties were Negroes. Negroes who married whites were guilty of a felony. Nowhere was the Negro permitted to hold public office, vote, serve on juries, or bear arms. Mississippi authorized "any person" to arrest and return to his employer any Negro who quit before the expiration of his contracted term of labor. Georgia warned that "all persons strolling about in idleness would be put in chain gangs and contracted out to employers." Thus, within a year following the end of the Civil War the Negro became the victim of white supremacy. The term "victim" is deliberately used since the legal tactics to "keep the Negro in his place" were often reinforced by extralegal tactics of violence and intimidation. Somewhat ironically, the fact that he was now free, no longer the property of some white man, made the Negro more vulnerable to the wanton and indiscriminate violence that was now directed against him by hoodlums from the "superior" race. There was, as John Hope Franklin has said, "an open season on Negroes."

This wave of terror and violence engulfed all who in any way undermined the scheme to keep whites superior. One group suspected of intentions to subvert white supremacy comprised the Yankee schoolteachers. These suspicions arose from the fact that these teachers had tried to impose "mixed schools" on the South, even though at that very moment segregated schools were common throughout the North. The whites refused to send their children to these Yankee "amalgamated" schools, forcing the Yankee schoolteachers to create, although reluctantly, the first de facto segregated schools for Negroes.

Faced with none but blacks in their classrooms, most of the Yankee teachers set about their job with missionary zeal. "Oh what a privilege to be among them when their morning dawns," wrote one teacher, "to see them personally coming forth from the land of Egypt and the house of bondage." Such enthusiasm evinced by these Yankees for the teaching of Negroes did nothing to allay the suspicions of the white Southerner. Yet often he was relieved, and shared the contemptuous amusement of his neighbors, when he found the Yankee schoolmarms—whose enthusiasm frequently outran their pedagogical sagacity—attempting to teach Latin and Greek to the newly freed slaves.

But this contemptuous amusement turned to fury when he discovered the Yankees teaching the blacks that they were the political and social equals of the whites. Nor was the white Southerner pleased to hear that the Negro was taught that the Northerners were his friends, that the Republican party was his benefactor, and that he should support his friends and benefactors at the ballot box. The Yankees often used ingenious political catechisms to accomplish their blatantly political aims. Here is a sample:

> "Now children you don't think white people are any better than you because they have straight hair and white faces?"
>
> "No, Sir."
>
> "No, they are no better, but they are different, they possess great power, they formed this great government, they control this vast country. . . . Now, what makes them different from you?"

"Money!" (unanimous shout).
"Yes, but what enabled them to obtain it? How did they get money?"
"Got it off us, stole it off we all."

Quite obviously the Southern whites were not going to tolerate this kind of education. And even the most tolerant white Southerner took umbrage when he heard former slaves singing "John Brown" or "Marching Through Georgia," songs taught him by the Yankee teachers. Increasingly then, these teachers had difficulty in getting hotel rooms or accommodations of any sort. Many restaurants refused to serve them. They were told not to attend church services. Corner louts hurled pleasantries after them, like "damned Yankee bitch of a nigger teacher." At times schools were burned, teachers flogged or driven out of town, usually after being tarred and feathered. In 1866 the Reverend J. P. Bardwell, American Missionary Association teacher at Grenada, Mississippi, was severely beaten, other teachers threatened, and an officer of the Freedmen's Bureau murdered.

Yet, despite the fact that white Southerners ostracized and sometimes attacked these Yankee teachers, there were some who approved of the education of the freedmen. A few white planters had actually set up schools for their black "hands." The education of the Negro was not opposed so much as was "outside interference." The Southerners wanted to control and supervise the education of *their* Negroes. Some Southern spokesmen for Negro education during this period argued that the Negro would be made "safer" if he were made "moral and intelligent," that is, if he were educated "Southern style." In addition to predictions that he would be safer (that is, constrained) if he were educated, there were predictions that he would be a better worker if educated. Some strategists went so far as to maintain that the Negro should vote, *provided that* the white man controlled, through education, his behavior at the ballot box. The rationale here was that the South might regain some of its political power nationally if it increased its number of voters by enfranchising the Negroes.

The white Southerner's interest in Negro education, however, was nothing compared with his interest in education for his own race. Education was the instrument for solving his problem. Whereas to the Northerner education had been the key to achieving reunion and reconstruction, to the Southern white education now became the key to white supremacy.

II

For the first time, the Southern states began to establish statewide systems of public education. Faced as they were at this period with problems of acute poverty and destitution, it is surprising that the state legislatures bothered at all with educational. matters. Yet bills setting up systems of education were passed in state after state throughout the South at the same time that laws were passed for the relief of debtors and allocations of money made to buy food for the starving. The rise of the public school system in the South at this difficult time indicates to what extent the freed Negro was considered a threat, for although the Black Codes had imposed legal constraints upon the Negro, making him subordinate to the white man, it was also necessary to ensure that these bonds could not be broken. The justification proffered for the Black Codes was that the Negro was ignorant, therefore not qualified to exercise the duties of citizenship. A corollary to this argument, of course, was that the white man was qualified to exercise the duties of citizenship because he was *not* ignorant. So to make this argument viable it became necessary to make plans to ensure the perpetuation of the ignorance of one race and the enlightenment of the other. Education would ensure that each race remained "in its place." All of the bills passed in the Southern states during the immediate postwar period reveal the strategy of constraining the Negro by curtailing his educational opportunities while at the same time providing liberal educational opportunities for whites. Texas set up a public school fund "exclusively for the education of white scholastics." Georgia's plan for the schooling of all from the ages of six to twenty-one was limited to "free white inhabitants." In 1867 Arkansas established a system of free public education "for whites only." In Tennessee the law provided for the maintenance of schools for not less than five months in the year "with separate schools for colored children." The state superintendent of education in Florida declared that the whites "had a deadly hatred to the education . . . of the freedmen." But Florida did make a concession to Negroes: If Negro males would pay a special tax of $1.25 per year, they could have their own public schools.

Secure in the conviction that the Black Codes had established white supremacy and that the educational plans would both perpetuate and justify it, the South now turned to the problem of "outside interference." The primary target was the Freedmen's Bureau. This agency of the federal government was a "curse," an "engine of mischief"; it was *the* symbol of outside interference. In their campaign against the Freedmen's Bureau the white Southerners had the support of the President of the United States, Andrew Johnson. A native of Tennessee, President Johnson, like every self-respecting

Southerner, had high regard for States' rights. When Congress passed a bill to extend the life and enlarge the functions of the bureau, he vetoed it. The bill, he declared, was "unnecessary, unwise, and unconstitutional."

Battle lines were now drawn between a President who contended to preserve the rights of the states and a Congress, dominated by so-called Radical Republicans, who contended to preserve the victory of Appomattox. The Radical Republicans were infuriated by the fact that less than two years after defeat most of the former Confederate states had established governments staffed exclusively by white men, who for the most part had been former leaders of the Confederacy. Congress' fight with the President culminated in a set of congressional resolutions that were to become the Fourteenth Amendment to the Constitution. This Amendment in effect declared Negroes citizens and then prescribed that: "No state shall abridge the privileges or immunities of citizens of the United States; nor shall any state deprive any person of life, liberty, or property, without due process of law; nor deny to any person within its jurisdiction, the equal protection of the laws." A second section penalized a state for withholding the privilege of voting by reducing its representation in Congress. A third section disqualified from office all rebels who had before the war taken the federal oath of office.

An amendment to the constitution has to be ratified by the states. What would the South do? The answer was not long in coming. Before the end of 1866 Texas, South Carolina, Georgia, Florida, North Carolina, Arkansas, and Alabama rejected the Fourteenth Amendment. In the first months of 1867 Virginia, Louisiana, and Mississippi turned it down. In the meantime the Northern states ratified it, led by Connecticut and New

Hampshire, both of whom approved it within a month.

The country once again was divided. Once more the Northerners were to champion the cause of the Negro against the Southern white. In March 1867, Congress made a dramatic move. After first declaring that there were no legal governments in the South, Congress ordered the South divided into five military districts, each in the charge of a military governor. Under the aegis of these military governors the rebel states were to form new constitutions framed by conventions of delegates elected by male citizens of "twenty-one years of age and upward, of whatever race, color or previous condition." One other stipulation was that the Fourteenth Amendment must be ratified. After the new state constitutions had been ratified by the electorate and approved by Congress, the states would be entitled to representation in Congress.

Once again the South had to bow to the North. Congressional Reconstruction effectively halted the South's attempt to restore white supremacy through Black Codes and discriminatory educational systems—at least for a time.

III

The most revolutionary aspect of Reconstruction was the entry of Negroes into the political arena, and at the moment Negroes became politically conscious, they focused attention on education. Just as the Yankee philanthropic societies had originally relied upon education to reconstruct the South and restore the Union, and just as the white southerners had tried to use education to perpetuate white supremacy, so now the Negroes saw education as the panacea for their problems.

The life of a slave under laws enforcing black illiteracy

was poor preparation for the Southern Negro for the responsibilities of citizenship. But education was the key; education could remedy all deficiencies, education could prepare all for effective participation. W. H. Grey, a Negro delegate to the Arkansas Constitutional Convention, exclaimed: "Give us the right of suffrage; establish a school system that will give us an opportunity to educate our children; leave ajar the door that leads to peace and power; and if by the next generation we do not place ourselves beyond the reach of mortal man, why then take them away from us if not exercised properly." In South Carolina, Negro delegate A. J. Ransier was more direct: "In proportion to the education of the people, so is their progress in civilization."

In their concern for the education of their race, many Negroes sought and secured important educational posts with the Reconstruction governments. In Louisiana, W. C. Brown was Superintendent of Public Instruction from 1872 to 1876. After serving a term as Secretary of State in Florida, Jonathan C. Gibbs, a Dartmouth graduate, became State Superintendent of Public Instruction. During Reconstruction Thomas Cardoza served as Mississippi's Superintendent of Education, while another Negro, Blanche K. Bruce, served as a county superintendent of schools before being sent to Congress in 1875 as one of that state's senators. From January 1873 to October 1874, J. C. Corbin, who had attended Oberlin, was Superintendent of Education in Arkansas. The post of Assistant Superintendent of Public Instruction in North Carolina was held for a time by James W. Hood.

Most Negro leaders saw that the responsibilities of citizenship required not only that the Negro be educated, but that he be educated together with whites. Segregated schools would stigmatize Negroes as second-class citizens, unequal to whites, and thus violate the Fourteenth Amendment. The Negro leaders also feared that if separate schools were established, Negro schools would be unequal to the white schools. So at every state constitutional convention held in the South during 1867–1868, the Negro delegates precipitated acrimonious debates on the "mixed school" question.

Most Southern whites dreaded racially mixed schools, fearful of the consequences of social intermixture. Many also doubted the educability of Negroes and saw mixed schools as pedagogically unsound. White opposition to mixed schools generated by these doubts and fears increased when it became evident that such schools would be supported almost completely by the white community. The burden of taxation, onerous in itself, became an insult to many whites when it was proposed that their money be used to support mixed schools.

The force of white opposition was so strong that in only two states, South Carolina and Louisiana, were Negroes able to secure constitutional guarantees for integrated schools. The Negro delegates were successful here only because they outnumbered the white delegates. All other state conventions were dominated by white majorities, but under the watchful eye of Congress none of these conventions tried to exclude Negroes from public education. Nor did any have the temerity to state explicitly that its publicly supported schools were to be segregated. There was little doubt that the Radical Republican Congress would reject such a restriction. Most states merely stipulated that education be provided for all children. At some conventions they added phrases like "without partiality or distinction," or "without distinction or preference." But such ambiguous phrases would not do, and the burden was shifted to the state assemblies where the issue of mixed schools was debated anew. Even here some sought to evade responsibility by permitting the local communities to decide. This move, of course, was violently opposed by the white citizens living in "black counties," where they were outnumbered by Negroes. In North Carolina the assembly ruled that the public schools of the state were to be segregated. In both Florida and Mississippi, where Negroes dominated the state legislatures, the decision went the other way; the legislatures maintained that the constitution be interpreted to support mixed schools.

One weakness of the mixed-school movement lay in the absence of compulsory education laws. In those four states where mixed schools were now required by law, the whites often refused to send their children to school at all. In Louisiana, for example, out of a school population of 253,000 in 1870, only 23,000 were reported to be in schools. In many communities—in Louisiana, South Carolina, Florida, and Mississippi—the laws were openly flouted by the creation of separate all-white schools.

Actually, within a few years the mixed school question all but disappeared as the white conservatives regained power in state after state. The earliest conservative victories occurred in Tennessee and Virginia in 1869, and in North Carolina the following year. Once restored to power, the conservatives in each state passed laws that explicitly provided for segregated schools. By 1875 Reconstruction had unofficially ended through conservative victories in all Southern states, save Louisiana, South Carolina, Florida, and Mississippi. In that year Congress moved to bolster its faltering program of Reconstruction by passing the Civil Rights Act.

In its original form this act included a provision that

prohibited segregated public schools. But it was removed before passage, and with its removal the movement for mixed schools collapsed. The man probably most singly responsible for the elimination was the Reverend Barnas Sears, General Agent for the Peabody Fund.

IV

In 1867 the munificent New Englander George Peabody gave the South $1 million. The money was to be used "for encouraging and promoting schools in those portions of our beloved and common country which have suffered from the destructive ravages and not less disastrous consequences of the civil war." The original board of trustees for the fund consisted of such distinguished names as U. S. Grant, Hamilton Fish, Governor of New York, and David Farragut, Tennessee-born Admiral of the United States Navy. Later elected trustees included Rutherford B. Hayes, Grover Cleveland, William McKinley, and Theodore Roosevelt. It is noteworthy that at all times one half of the board of trustees were Southerners.

In setting up this fund, Peabody granted the trustees the freedom to decide how the money was to be distributed. The trustees, in turn, delegated most policy-making to their first general agent, the Reverend Barnas Sears.

Barnas Sears had a rich educational background to prepare him for his work with the Peabody Fund. He had succeeded Horace Mann, "The Father of the Common School," as Secretary of the Massachusetts State Board of Education. Before that he had been State Superintendent of Normal Schools in Massachusetts. At the time he was asked to become the general agent for the Peabody Fund Barnas Sears was serving as president of Brown University.

The educational fund he administered rarely yielded more than $90,000 a year, occasionally as much as $130,000. As general agent, Sears' strategy was to use this small amount of money to stimulate the South to support its own public schools. To accomplish this end, he decided that all funds should be dispersed on a matching basis. Rather than pay for the entire expense of a school or institute, only a small portion, usually one fourth, was supplied by the fund. This meant that the Peabody money was spread very thinly throughout the South. The largest donation to any state in one year, from 1868 to 1914, was $37,975—to Virginia in 1874.

Two notable consequences followed from this policy of granting money on a matching basis. First, the only localities able to match the grants were usually the larger towns and cities. The indirect discrimination against rural areas was all the more unfortunate since this is where most of the school-age children lived. Second, and more important, this policy reinforced segregated schooling in the South. Sears condemned mixed schools and refused to aid them, on the grounds that the white people would not support them, hence would not provide funds to match a Peabody grant. In Louisiana he gave no aid to the public schools, giving instead grants to the private white schools. When criticized for this action, Sears replied that he was helping the white children of Louisiana because they were "the most destitute from the fact of their unwillingness to attend mixed schools." He added that "colored children would likewise be given preference, were they in like circumstances."

Not only did he reinforce the principle and practice

of segregated education by refusing aid to integrated schools with Peabody's money, but Sears persuaded others against mixed schools. Taking a special trip to Washington in 1873, Sears appeared before the leading members of Congress to plead against the prohibition of segregated schools contained in the Civil Rights Act. He succeeded in convincing them, he later reported, "that the bill would overthrow the state systems of free schools and leave both the blacks and whites . . . destitute of schools altogether."

Undoubtedly the Peabody Fund and its indefatigable first general agent were the catalysts that helped stimulate Southerners to build, support, and control their own public schools. In accomplishing this work, the Peabody Fund had departed from the usual pattern of Northern philanthropy with its paternalistic concern with private, church, or missionary schools. And yet the Peabody Fund in the long run intensified the South's educational problem, for, although at that time the white Southerner would neither support nor attend mixed schools, the alternative of segregated schools increased the financial burden and prevented the South from attaining educational equality with the North for the next seventy-five years.

And what about the Southern Negro? What about his vision of education as the key to acceptance? The Negro had believed that the condition of subordination of his race was remediable. Once educated like the white man, he would be accepted by the white man. But now, before Reconstruction had officially ended, these plans had been undermined by the establishment of segregated schools. With the passage of the Civil Rights Act in 1875 the Negro's faith in education was visibly shaken, as evidenced by the decline in school enrollment. In Arkansas

Negro enrollment decreased from 73,878 in 1875 to 15,890 in 1876. In Florida it fell from 32,371 in 1875 to 26,052 the following year. Though weakened, the faith of the Negro in education did not disappear. At root he still believed in its magical power—else what had he to hope for? Even though he had to settle for segregated schools, at least he had schools, schools that were on the whole as good as those for white children. Now concern shifted to the problem of preserving that equality. The conservatives in all of the Southern states had pledged to maintain parity between white and black schools. It was on the strength of this pledge that many Negroes actually cast their votes to return the conservatives to power. Would the pledge be honored?

V

When President Hayes removed the last of the federal troops from the South in 1877, Reconstruction was officially over. Segregated schools were by now a fact of life in the South, but although the Negro attended separate schools and separate churches (here by choice), he was not totally segregated from the white man's world. Tolerance and acceptance of the Negro were widespread in many areas of public life in the South. There was neither segregation nor separation on trains or streetcars, or at the polls, in the courts and legislatures, on the police force, or in the militia. A Negro newspaperman from Boston reported from Columbia, South Carolina, in 1885 that he felt about as safe there as in Providence, Rhode Island. Throughout the South, he reported, "I can ride in first class cars on the railroads and in the streets. I can go into saloons and get refreshments even as in New York. I can stop in and drink a glass of soda and be more politely waited upon than in some parts of New England."

It is true, of course, that the Negro at this time was held subordinate to the white man and frequently exploited by him. But white supremacy did not, then, mean the degradation of the Negro—he was not ostracized, he was not disenfranchised, he was not totally segregated.

The position the Negro held in the South during this period was largely due to the white conservatives. Since their coming to power marked the end of Reconstruction, this first generation of conservatives liked to be called the "Redeemers." They were neither Negrophobes nor Negrophiles. Descendants of the ante-bellum slaveholders, they preached an aristocratic philosophy of paternalism and noblesse oblige. As Governor Thomas G. Jones of Alabama bluntly put it: "The Negro race is under us. He is in our power. We are his custodians . . . we should extend to him as far as possible all the civil rights that will fit him to be a decent and self-respecting, law-abiding, and intelligent citizen. . . . If we do not lift them up, they will drag us down."

But the power of the conservatives was not to go unchallenged. The Civil War had done more than emancipate the Negro slave; it had emancipated the whites of the lower economic class. Small farmers and tradesmen, from the hill country and beyond, fought against this return to the power structure of ante-bellum days. During the war and its aftermath they had tasted power for the first time. They did not intend to again be the charges, or the victims, of the aristocracy.

There was one sure way for the lower-class whites to guarantee themselves freedom and autonomy. The key, once more, was education. Free, universal education would make them the equal of the aristocratic conservatives. The laws had been passed; in many cases the schools had been built and the teachers hired. They need only take advantage of what already existed. The increase in school enrollments tells the story. In 1880 there were 1,053,025 white children enrolled in the public schools. In the next fifteen years, from 1880 to 1895, white school enrollment more than doubled.

	WHITE ENROLLMENT	NEGRO ENROLLMENT
1880	1,053,025	714,884
1885	1,378,926	835,053
1890	1,864,214	1,026,947
1895	2,176,464	1,142,500

Increased school enrollment was only half the educational picture. The other half—the half that brings into perspective the power struggle between the two white economic classes—is the sorry condition of financial support, for despite the increased educational responsibility, we find all states spending less for education. In Alabama $523,799 was spent for education in 1875 but only $375,645 in 1880. Louisiana's expenditure decreased from $699,655 in 1875 to $486,320. In South Carolina it went from $426,640 to $324,679. Over this five-year period the South's educational expenditures decreased approximately 21 percent, while enrollment had increased 33 percent.

Part of the explanation for this reduction in expenditures for education at the very time school enrollment was increasing lies in the fact that the aristocrats in power had no personal interest in the public schools. Traditionally they had educated their children in private schools, and this continued to be the case until the mid-eighties. Public schools for the masses, therefore, did not have widespread support among the class in power. William L. Royall, the editor of the Richmond *Common-*

wealth, wrote in 1880 that education beyond the barest rudiments was "imported here by a gang of carpetbaggers." He added that taxation to support such education was socialistic. It should be provided, he felt, "for pauper children only, as before the war." The Governor of Virginia, F. W. M. Holliday, agreed, explaining that the public schools were "a luxury . . . to be paid for like any other luxury, by the people who wish their benefits."

The conservatives' lack of support for the public schools was not due solely to their own selfish interests. They had regained power after Reconstruction partly by pledging themselves to a program of financial retrenchment. They promised to "spend nothing unless absolutely necessary." These Redeemers had adopted retrenchment to counter both the extravagance of the Reconstruction government and the depression that had gripped the South ever since the panic of 1873. During the first decade of "home rule," cheap government became widely accepted as the criterion of good government. As Governor George F. Drew of Florida said to his legislature in 1877, "that government will be the most highly esteemed that gives the greatest protection to the taxpayer."

Retrenchment meant reduced salaries for all state officials. It also meant a curtailment in all state services, and the first service to suffer was public education. Actually, the Redeemers did more than reduce education expenditures—they put a strait jacket on them. Fearful that Negroes or carpetbaggers might regain political power, the conservatives set up checks against the possible misuse of such power. They did this by adopting constitutional prohibitions against local taxation for schools, by placing constitutional limitations upon the state legislatures with regard to the rate of taxation that they could

levy for school purposes, and by limiting the amount of
money that could be appropriated for the support of
public schools. So determined were the conservatives to
guard against Negro and carpetbagger power, they fashioned "change proof" state constitutions, thereby making
it almost impossible for the lower economic classes among
the whites to change the constitutions to extend support
for free schools.

The small farmers, sparked by the newly formed
Grange and later by the Farmers Alliance, continued to
agitate for the extension of public schools. They clamored
for local taxation, they wanted an increase in the state
fund. In both these demands they were constricted by
the state constitutions and opposed by the planter aristocrats from the lowlands. In desperation the small farmers
turned to the matter of distribution of state funds. They
wanted to divert some of the money intended for Negro
education to the white schools. But this demand for
abolishing the system of distribution according to per
capita school population was also vetoed by the conservatives, who continued to honor their pledge that they
would maintain the schools of the Negroes on an equality
with those of white children.

Yet as long as the Negro had no *real* political power,
diversion of school funds from black to white children
was inevitable—despite all pledges. In fact the conservatives themselves became the leaders in this strategy of
diversion. By the mid-eighties many of the upper-class
planters were beginning to send their children to the
public schools. Since these aristocrats lived in "black
counties," that is, counties where Negroes outnumbered
whites, it was possible, as Horace Mann Bond has shown,
"to divert some part of the per capita funds intended
for Negro education to the improvement of the schools

for white children *without altering the per capita distribution given by the state to each county.*" This strategy was first adopted in Mississippi with the help of a teaching certificate law of 1886 that permitted separate salary scales for the two races. From 1877 to 1885 the average monthly salaries of teachers of both races in Mississippi had been identical. With the passage of the certificate law Negro salaries began to fall, white salaries to rise. In 1886 the monthly average for white teachers was $31.37, for Negro teachers $27.40. By 1895 white teachers were earning $33.04 per month, Negro teachers $21.46.

This strategy of diverting funds to white schools was feasible only in the "black counties" since in the "white counties" where the whites were more than a majority, there could be little financial gain to the white schools if a part of the per capita fund for Negro education was diverted. This caused many of the small farmers of the white counties to grow increasingly bitter over what they took to be an unjust situation. In their own counties they paid most, if not all, the taxes, but their schools were inferior to those for whites in the "black counties." Since the money spent for Negro education was held to be the reason for the superiority of the white schools in the "black counties," *and* the reason for inferior schools for whites in the "white counties," some whites now began to question the feasibility of Negro education. Demagogues seized upon the issue and went before their constituents to argue against the education of Negroes at public expense, or at least in favor of the division of the school fund on the basis of the tax paid by the two races. Here they were always opposed by the white leaders of the "black counties" who had a vested interest in the continuation of the equitable allocation of state funds for Negro education—such funds being used in part to improve their own white schools.

The culmination of this struggle between the white economic classes, in which the Negro was used as a pawn, came in the nineties with the rise of Populism. The Populist movement in the South articulated the resentment of the small farmer against the old aristocracy. In this political battle the Populists attempted to win the allegiance of the Negro. Appealing to the kinship of common grievances, Tom Watson told the Negroes that "the colored tenant is in the same boat with the white tenant, the colored laborer with the white laborer." Negroes were promised that "if you stand up for your rights and for your manhood, if you stand shoulder to shoulder with us in this fight" the People's party will "wipe out the color line and put every man on his citizenship irrespective of color." Actually, with the Populists racial integration went further than it ever had with the conservatives. Negroes served with Southern whites as members of state, district, and county executive committees of the party; they served on campaign committees and were delegates to national conventions. Black and white candidates had places on official party tickets. Audiences of both races heard black and white campaigners speaking from the same platform. According to C. Vann Woodward, "The Negroes responded with more enthusiasm and hope than to any other political movement." And he adds, "it is altogether probable that during the brief Populist upheaval of the nineties Negroes and whites achieved a greater comity of mind and harmony of political purpose than ever before or since in the South." This precarious experiment in interracial harmony, handicapped by suspicion and prejudice, surprised everyone by the good will and cooperation it generated between the races—for a time.

The honeymoon ended when the Populists' bid for political power failed. By using every means at their disposal—including fraud, intimidation, bribery, violence, and terror—the conservatives won the election of 1896. This defeat generated such dismay among the Populists that a scapegoat had to be found to explain away the failure. One was ready at hand: the Negro. Alliance with him, white Populists claimed, had alarmed many in the South who would have voted for their cause, but did not because they feared "Negro domination." The Negro was blamed for the political fiasco, and the biracial partnership was dissolved.

The outlook for the Negro was dim indeed, for not only the Populists but the conservatives as well had now abandoned entirely the cause of the Negro. In battling for their political lives, the conservatives had forsaken the stance of paternalistic protector of the Negro and had moved into the camp of the Negrophobes. Alarmed by the success the Populists were obtaining with their appeal to the Negro voter, the conservatives had raised the cry of "Negro Domination." Now that they had won their election—in part through the support of extremists—the conservatives saw no reason to go back on their militant platform of white supremacy. All the more so because this platform could now be used to build a rapprochement with the white Populists.

Repudiated by his sometime friends in the South, the Negro by this time found few friendly voices in the North. For a variety of reasons the commitment of many Northern liberals to racial equality had been considerably exhausted. Some liberals who had started out with a highly romanticized concept of the Negro experienced disenchantment with the freedmen. Others extended the economic and political doctrine of laissez faire to this area: according to this view the "Negro problem" was the South's problem and could best be solved by the South, without "outside interference." Still other liberals, in response to the political turmoils of the recent past, deplored sectional animosities, for example, those between the North and the South, and identified those who exploited them as reactionaries and demagogues. Drawn toward the cause of sectional reconciliation, the liberals came to see the Negro as the symbol of sectional strife. Thus, for a variety of reasons, Northern liberals gave up their role of protector of the Negro, and some even went so far as to begin mouthing the shibboleth of white supremacy.

As white supremacy gradually became "the American way," the highest court in the land proceeded to give it legal sanctions. As early as 1877 the United States Supreme Court had ruled that a state could not *prohibit* segregation on a common carrier. The Court in 1890 ruled that a state could constitutionally *require* segregation on carriers. In 1896 in *Plessy v. Ferguson* the Court declared that "legislation is powerless to eradicate racial instincts." In this decision it provided the justification for segregation by its enunciation of the doctrine of "separate but equal." Two years later in *Williams v. Mississippi* the Court approved the Mississippi plan for depriving Negroes of the vote, completing in the words of Woodward "the opening of the legal road to proscription, segregation, and disfranchisement."

All the stops were out. The Negro was now an approved object of aggression. The way was clear for a capitulation to racism. It had been cleared by the sanctions of the federal courts, by the Northern liberals eager to conciliate the South, by Southern conservatives who had abandoned their policy of protector of the Negro in their struggle against the Populists, and finally by the Populists in their mood of disillusionment with their former Negro allies.

The first step was the total disfranchisement of the Negro. The first state to disfranchise on a racial basis and evade the restrictions of the federal constitution was Mississippi. Other Southern states followed. The plan was to set up certain barriers, such as property or literacy qualifications, or payment of a poll tax, then cut certain loopholes "through which only white men could squeeze." The loopholes to accommodate the underprivileged whites were the "understanding clause," the "grandfather clause," and the "good character clause."

Some idea of the effectiveness of disfranchisement can be had from a comparison of the number of Negro voters in Louisiana in 1896, when there were 130,334 and in 1904, when there were 1,342. The literacy, property, and poll tax qualifications had done their work well. In 1896 Negro registrants were a majority in twenty-six parishes —by 1900 in none.

In conjunction with the device of disfranchisement, the policies of segregation and discrimination were extended by the adoption of a great number of Jim-Crow laws. Separation of the races on all public carriers— trains, streetcars, steamboats—became the law throughout the South. Signs bearing the legends "White Only" or "Colored" appeared over the portals of theaters, boarding houses, waiting rooms, and toilets, over ticket windows and water fountains.

Disfranchised, segregated, and ostracized, the Negro was held to be incapable of self-government, unworthy of the franchise, and impossible to educate beyond the rudiments. The rudiments cost little, and little indeed was spent for Negro education. In 1907 Mississippi spent $5.02 per child for the education of white children, for Negro children the figure was $1.10. In some counties of Mississippi ("black counties"), as much as $30 to $38 was spent for each white child while expenditures for Negro children ranged from 27 cents to a dollar. In Alabama by 1909 there was a 514.8 percent excess of white expenditures over Negro expenditures per capita; in other words, for every dollar of public school funds allotted to a Negro child in 1909, $6.14 was received by a white child. Everywhere there was the contemptuous rejection of Negro education as something that would make him unfit for work. Even those who devoted time and effort to Negro education were pessimistic about his educability. A professor from the University of Virginia said in 1900 that "the Negro race is essentially a race of peasant farmers and laborers. . . . As a source of cheap labor for a warm climate he is beyond competition; everywhere else he is a foreordained failure."

And the Negro—what was his role in this oppression? The resistance of the Negro himself has long ceased to be a deterrent to white aggression. And by the nineties, when the "new South" was beginning to emerge, a Negro leader came forward to preach a philosophy that tended to undermine Negro resistance and helped smooth the path to proscription. Once more education was to be the answer to the Negro's problems. But the new spokesman for his people declared that the Negroes required a different kind of education from that given to white men. The education of the Negro, said Booker T. Washington, "should make the Negro humble, simple, and of service to the community."

VI

Born a slave in Virginia in 1856, Booker T. Washington knew poverty intimately. His bed as a child was a heap of old rags on a dirt floor. When the Civil War ended young Booker was taken by his mother to Malden, West Virginia, where his stepfather worked in a salt furnace. Their new cabin, he tells us, was worse than the one he had lived in as a slave. Home was in the midst of a cluster of cabins jammed close together with no sanitary regulations, so that "the filth about the cabin was often intolerable." Negroes and whites—"the poorest and most ignorant and degenerate white people"—lived crowded together with much drinking, gambling, quarreling, and fighting. Washington, though only a child, went to work with his stepfather in one of the salt furnaces. While working by day, young Washington attended school at night where, with the help of a succession of itinerant Negro teachers and his own determination, he learned to read and write. He continued his night schooling when he left the salt furnace to work in a local coal mine, and even later when he left the mine to become a servant in the home of the mine owner. Mrs. Viola Ruffner, wife of the mine owner, was a "Yankee woman" from Vermont with a reputation for being very strict with her servants. But Washington reported that the lessons he learned in the home of Mrs. Ruffner were "as valuable . . . as any education I have ever gotten anywhere since." He got along with her because he quickly learned what she wanted: "first of all she wanted everything kept clean about her . . . she

wanted things done promptly and systematically, and
. . . at the bottom of everything she wanted absolute
honesty and frankness."

Despite his success at Mrs. Ruffner's, Washington
wanted to go to Hampton Institute, a school for Negroes
he had heard about while working in the mine. So in
1872, at the age of sixteen, he left Malden to make the
500-mile trip to Virginia. He had $1.50 in his pocket, and
when he arrived at Hampton, his ragged condition almost kept him from being admitted to the school. He was
finally given an entrance examination: sweeping the
recitation room.

> I swept the recitation room three times. Then I got a
> dusting-cloth and I dusted it four times. All the wood-
> work around the walls, every bench, table and desk,
> I went over four times with my dusting-cloth. Besides,
> every piece of furniture had been moved and every
> closet and corner in the room had been thoroughly
> cleaned. I had the feeling that in a large measure my
> future depended upon the impression I made upon
> the teacher in the cleaning of that room. When I was
> through, I reported to the head teacher. She was a
> "Yankee" woman who knew just where to look for
> dirt. She went into the room and inspected the floor
> and the closets; then she took her handkerchief and
> rubbed it on the woodwork about the walls, and over
> the table and benches. When she was unable to find
> one bit of dirt on the floor, or a particle of dust on
> any of the furniture, she quietly remarked, "I guess
> you will do to enter this institution."

Hampton Institute had been founded by General
Samuel Chapman Armstrong shortly after the war. Armstrong was convinced that the only hope for the future
of the South "lay in a vigorous attempt to lift the colored

race by a practical education that would fit them for life."
The instruction given at Hampton consisted of manual
training. But this education of the hands of the Negroes
was not intended merely to increase their wage-earning
capacity. Manual training, in the mind of General Armstrong, was not just economically desirable; he saw in
labor, in physical work, a spiritual force—"a force that
promoted fidelity, honesty, accuracy, persistence, and intelligence." A practical education, as he conceived it,
disciplined the mind and formed character and at the
same time made a man economically efficient.

At Hampton, General Armstrong taught selected Negroes to respect labor, especially skilled labor, and to appreciate the values such work had in the formation of
character. If education was to be effective for life, he
counseled, it must be like the conduct of life itself, "both
alert and patient, beginning where the *pupil was*, and
creating character rather than comfort, goodness rather
than goods." In keeping with his conception of education as character training, Armstrong insisted that education must be "won rather than given." And once he had
an education, the Negro was to perform some useful
service, some task that the world wanted. Education
"must inspire the will to serve rather than the will to
get; it must be a struggle, not for life alone, but for the
lives of others."

In his autobiography, Washington says that of the two
greatest benefits he received from Hampton Institute, the
first was "contact with a great man, General S. C. Armstrong . . . the rarest, strongest, and most beautiful character that it has ever been my privilege to meet." The
second benefit was to learn what education was expected
to do for an individual; that is, he "not only learned that
it was not a disgrace to labor, but learned to love labor,

not alone for its financial value, but for labor's own sake and the independence and self-reliance which the ability to do something which the world wants done brings."

After graduating from Hampton Institute in 1875, Washington returned to his home in Malden, to teach in the same school he had attended just a few years before. In 1878 to further his education he enrolled in Wayland Seminary in Washington, D.C. The year he spent in the capital confirmed Washington in the beliefs and ideas he had already distilled from his earlier experiences. At this school he found that the students, in most cases, had more money, were better dressed, and in some cases were more brilliant mentally, than the students at Hampton. But he also found that the Seminary students were less self-dependent and seemed to give more attention to outward appearances. The crucial difference, he noted, was that "they did not appear to me to be beginning at the bottom, on a real solid foundation, to the extent that they were at Hampton." In a significant afterthought he added that "they were not as much inclined as the Hampton students to go into the county districts of the South, where there was little comfort, to take up work for our people." In Washington, D.C., he also met scores of Negroes who had held government positions during the Reconstruction period. Unemployed and often impoverished, this class of Negroes greatly alarmed Washington by the attention they paid to keeping up appearances and by their seeming dependence upon the government "for every conceivable thing." Once again he was confirmed in his belief that the Negro must build upon a solid foundation—a foundation in education, industry, and property.

After his year at Wayland Seminary, Washington returned to Hampton Institute as an instructor. He first served there as a house father to a group of Indian students who were brought to Hampton as an experiment. Later he was put in charge of the new night-school program that was started for deserving students. Then in the spring of 1881, Washington took up the career that was to be his life's work. Upon the recommendation of General Armstrong he was offered the job of starting a normal school for Negro teachers that was to be established in Tuskegee, Alabama.

Most of the month of June, Washington spent traveling through Alabama, visiting with the Negro families of the state. Talking with them and living with them convinced him more than ever of "the wisdom of the system that General Armstrong had inaugurated at Hampton." Washington had learned well the General's dictum that education must begin where the pupil was. To take the children of such people as he had been among for a month, Washington thought, and give them each day a few hours of mere book education, "would be almost a waste of time." The new head of Tuskegee Normal Institute had no high regard for book learning—not for his people, not at that time. He revealed that one of the "saddest things" he saw during that month of travel "was a young man, who had attended some high school, sitting down in a one-room cabin, with grease on his clothing, filth all around him, and weeds in the yard and garden, engaged in studying French Grammar."

The Tuskegee students, he noted, came from homes where they had no opportunity to learn how to care for their bodies. He wanted to teach these students how to bathe, how to care for their teeth. (Washington was convinced that "there were few single agencies of civilization that are more far reaching than the toothbrush.") He wanted to teach them what to eat, and how to eat it properly, how to care for their clothing and their rooms. Aside from this he wanted to give them "such a practical knowledge of some one industry, together with the spirit of industry, thrift and economy, that they would be sure of knowing how to make a living after they had left." Finally, since 85 percent of the Negroes in the Gulf states depended upon agriculture for their livelihood, he wanted his graduates "to return to the plantation districts and show the people there how to put new energy and new ideas into farming, as well as into the intellectual and moral and religious life of the people."

At Tuskegee, Washington attempted to apply the doctrines of General Armstrong beyond the walls of Hampton Institute, to apply those doctrines to all Negroes. As Washington saw it, the Negro had one basic problem: to win the respect of the white man. The solution to this problem was simple: practice thrift, industry, and honesty and the white man would respect you. Washington's personal success—from his job as servant boy in the home of Mrs. Ruffner to his position as the principal of Tuskegee Institute—attested to the efficacy of those virtues. Negroes, he taught, should buy homes and farms, establish themselves in even the humblest of occupations. Through their good works as members of the community they would win over the white man.

Booker T. Washington accepted and strongly believed in a society of merit. He was convinced that the Negro had to earn acceptance into the larger American society. He was equally convinced that the Negro could win such acceptance. Education—"Tuskegee style"—was the key to acceptance. Once the Negro community had been infused with the Protestant ethic of thrift, industry, and honesty, acceptance would come.

With the help of his students, of Northern white

philanthropists, and his own drive to succeed, Washington made Tuskegee a showplace for Negro education. In 1893 he delivered a memorial address at Hampton Institute in honor of the late General Armstrong. On this occasion he pointed out how Tuskegee Institute had been founded on the belief that the Negro must be helped to help himself, a lesson Washington indicated he had learned from the General himself. Washington took this opportunity to recount proudly the achievements of Tuskegee Institute:

> Eleven years ago Tuskegee was one of hundreds of similar villages scattered through the Gulf States. Today it is the lighthouse for that section. Eleven years ago there were 30 students and one teacher; now there are 600 students and 38 teachers; then scarcely a dollar and not a foot of land; now 1,400 acres of land, 20 buildings, and real and personal property worth $180,000; then one blind horse; now 260 head of livestock. Then the plantation where the Tuskegee Institute stood had known nought but the labor forced by lash; today there are 19 industries kept in motion by 600 as happy hearts as can be found in America; then some feared that the Negro youth would be ashamed to work for his education, but these students have made and laid into the buildings with their own hands 2,000,000 bricks, and of 20 buildings, 17 have been built and furnished by the students themselves (*Selected Speeches*).

Over the years Booker T. Washington became known nationally. In 1884 in an address he gave to the National Education Association he said, "the whole future of the Negro rested largely upon the question as to whether or not he should make himself, through his skill, intelligence and character, of such undeniable value to the community in which he lived that the community could not dispense with his presence." The following year Washington was elected president of the Alabama State Teachers Association. The apex of his career came in 1895 when he delivered the opening address at the Cotton State Exposition in Georgia. The invitation to deliver the speech as well as the warm reception given him signified white recognition of him as the spokesman for his race. In his first declaration as that spokesman Washington told the white Southerners in his audience that the Negro did not want social equality, that he did not need social equality with the whites. Nor did he want, or need, political or civil equality. To the Negroes in his audience, Washington emphasized the necessity of cooperation with their white friends. Negro education, he proclaimed, should be devoted to the practical education of earning a living. To both whites and blacks Washington preached conciliation and harmony between the races. Holding up his hand, with his fingers wide apart, he exclaimed, "in all things purely social we can be as separate as the fingers, yet one as the hand in all things essential to mutual progress."

The response of the white Southerners to this speech was electric. When he finished speaking, Washington found that Governor R. F. Bullock had rushed across the stage and was shaking his hand. The handshaking, back-thumping, and hearty congratulations were such that Washington had difficulty getting out of the building. Papers in all parts of the United States published the address in full, and for months afterwards there were complimentary editorial references to it. The editor of the *Atlanta Constitution* wrote, in part: "I do not exaggerate when I say that Professor Booker T. Washington's address yesterday was one of the most notable speeches, both as to character and as to the warmth of its reception, ever delivered to a southern audience. The address was a revelation. The whole speech is a platform upon which blacks and whites can stand with full justice to each other." A few days after the Atlanta address Washington received a congratulatory message from Grover Cleveland, the President of the United States.

Perhaps the most poignant comment of all came from a reporter of the *New York World*, who noted that at the end of the speech "most of the Negroes in the audience were crying, perhaps without knowing just why." Among the Negroes, after an initial burst of enthusiasm, there gradually began to grow the suspicion that they had been sold out. The Atlanta address soon came to be referred to as the "Atlanta Compromise." Actually, the speech at Atlanta was no departure from Washington's earlier doctrine. From the earliest he had preached to his fellow Negroes: "Make yourself useful to the South; be honest, be thrifty; cultivate the white man's friendliness; above all, educate your children and prepare them for the future." Nor did Washington abrogate social, political, or civil equality at Atlanta. What he said was that such equality "must be the result of a severe and constant struggle." The words and sentiments expressed at Atlanta in 1895 were not new. What was new was the acceptance by a white audience of these as the words and sentiments of the Negro race. But most important of all to the Negroes was the fact that this speech, in its enthusiastic endorsement by the white Southerner, occurred at the very moment the Negro was being disfranchised, segregated, and deprived of his social, civil, and political rights.

Washington's whole program was grounded on the assumption that America was a society of merit. If the

Negro acquired certain habits, the habits of a free man, which would enable him to become independent and self-sufficient—both in his inner life and in his work—then the Negro would increasingly gain civil equality. What Washington did not count on was the political debacle which induced the Southern conservatives to desert the Negro in order to subordinate class conflict among whites. Once this took place, Washington's program was undermined. No matter how honest, thrifty, and industrious he might become, the Negro was destined to be proscribed, segregated, and disfranchised. America, for the Negro, was no longer a society of merit.

In spite of the empirical reality confronting him, Washington continued to believe. In 1900 he wrote: "I am conscious of the fact that mere connection with what is known as a superior race will not permanently carry an individual to reward unless he has individual worth, and mere connection with what is regarded as an inferior race will not finally hold an individual back if he possess intrinsic, individual merit." This belief was shared by many of his people. When in 1913 the Negroes celebrated their fiftieth year of emancipation, many saw the celebrations and expositions commemorating a half century's progress as testimonials to the teachings of Washington. The statistics for the "year of jubilee" were impressive; in 1913 there were 138,557 Negro farm owners and 550,000 Negro homeowners. In 1900 Washington had organized the Negro Business League. By 1913 there were 38,000 Negro business enterprises, and Washington could point with pride to these self-made black capitalists as the heroes of their race—success had come to them through their industry, their thrift, their honesty. The total wealth of American Negroes was estimated at $700,-000,000. Perhaps most impressive of all was the reduction of Negro illiteracy. In 1845 over 90 percent of the Negroes were illiterate; by 1913 this figure had been reduced to 30 percent.

At the very moment Washington was receiving testimonials, the voices of his critics were becoming more strident. The educational gains were laudable, they admitted, but where was the educated Negro elite, the "talented tenth" necessary to lead the masses to social, political, and civil equality? Washington's level of aspiration had been too low. William E. B. Du Bois poured vitriolic scorn on Washington's educational program in a speech at Hampton Institute: "Take the eyes of the millions off the stars and fasten them in the soil and if their young men will dream dreams, let them be dreams of corn bread and molasses."

And the material gains of the Negro? This idea too was praiseworthy, the critics admitted, but look at the price that had to be paid. Washington, they insisted, had sold the human dignity of the Negro for a few crumbs of material wealth. The need was not for material wealth, but for justice—political, civil, and social justice.

VII

The man who emerged as the leader of these critics was William E. B. Du Bois. Du Bois, however, never retained that mantle with the tenacity of his predecessor. In fact, Du Bois successively alienated white liberals and Negroes, finally losing almost all influence on his race.

It would be difficult to imagine two men more strikingly different than William E. B. Du Bois and Booker T. Washington. Even the conditions surrounding their birth and early lives were markedly different. Washington was born a slave in West Virginia; Du Bois was born a free man in the town of Great Barrington, Massachusetts, a community in which the color line was so faint that for all practical purposes, Du Bois grew up in an integrated community. Unlike Washington, who never knew who his father was, Du Bois could trace his family back to the period of the American Revolution. The wretched poverty of Washington's youth was matched by the genteel poverty of Du Bois' childhood. Perhaps the most glaring contrast between the two men was their educational background. Washington's formal schooling was on a catch-as-catch-can basis until he entered Hampton Institute at the age of sixteen. Du Bois had received one of the finest educations of any man of his period; he had taken the classical course in high school, after which he spent three years at Fisk University, going then to Harvard University where he received a Doctor of Philosophy degree. He finished his studies with two years at the University of Berlin. As might be expected the personalities of these two men were a study in contrasts. Washington's warm, outgoing ways prompted someone once to describe him as looking like a farmer dressed up in his Sunday clothes. But this "Sunday clothes farmer" was a master diplomat, a born leader, with the knack of pleasing everybody. The cold, austere, even haughty countenance of Du Bois was reminiscent of a Spanish aristocrat, an image reinforced by his Vandyke beard. For his first job at Wilberforce College in Ohio, Du Bois arrived on the scene bedecked in a silk hat, gloves, spats, and swinging a cane. Nobody looked less like a farmer! If Washington was the diplomat who pleased everybody, Du Bois became the critic who alienated everybody.

From the years 1894 to 1910 Du Bois was an academician, teaching first at Wilberforce and then at Atlanta University. The relationship between the two men was cordial at first, but gradually tension developed. In 1902 Du Bois published a book, *The Souls of Black Folk,* containing an essay on Booker T. Washington. He called Washington the most distinguished Southerner since Jefferson Davis. But, he went on: "Washington asked the Negro to give up, at least for the present, three things: political power, insistence on civil rights, and higher education of Negro youth." Then Du Bois posed the question: "As a result of this tender of the palm branch, what has been the return?" The return, according to Du Bois, was threefold: the Negro had been disfranchised; he had been allocated a distinct status of civil inferiority; and aid to institutions of higher education had been steadily withdrawn. It should be noted that Du Bois did not attribute these developments directly to Washington's teachings, but he said, "his propaganda has, without a shadow of a doubt, helped their speedier accomplishment." So at this point in time there was not an outright repudiation of Washington, but the lines were clearly drawn, as can be seen in the following quote:

> So far as Mr. Washington preaches Thrift, Patience and Industrial Training for the Masses, we must hold up his hands and strive with him, rejoicing in his honors and glorying in the strength of the Joshua called of God and of man to lead the headless host. But, so far as Mr. Washington apologizes for injustice, North, or South, does not rightly value the privilege and duty of voting, belittles the emasculating effects of caste distinction, and opposes the higher training and ambition of our brighter minds, so far as he, the South, or the Nation does this—we must unceasingly and firmly oppose them.

No one who read those words could help but conclude that the Negroes now had another brilliant, articulate spokesman, one more forceful, more aggressive, more militant than Booker T. Washington. The difference between the two leaders was one of emphasis. Du Bois represented the new exclusive concern of the Negro with his rights. What was missing was Washington's concern with the Negro community. An industrious, honest, thrifty community was a prerequisite, he taught, to the granting of those rights. Du Bois and his followers vigorously rejected the notion that the Negro had to win his rights and denied that these rights were granted only to those who merited them. "By every civilized and peaceful method," Du Bois wrote, "we must strive for the rights which the world accords to men, clinging unwaveringly to those great words which the sons of the Fathers would fain forget: 'We hold these truths to be self-evident: That all men are created equal; that they are endowed by their creator with certain inalienable rights; that among these are life, liberty and the pursuit of happiness.' "

In 1910 Du Bois left Atlanta University and went to New York to become Director of Research for the recently formed National Association for the Advancement of Colored People (NAACP), and editor of its magazine, Crisis. For the next fifty years the role of leader was taken over by this organization. The cult of personality disappeared. Du Bois himself was overshadowed by the organization. He left it once in 1934 after he advocated racial separation, abandoning the association's goal of an integrated society. He later returned, but embraced socialism which led to his second and final break with the NAACP in 1948. From that time until his death in 1963 Du Bois moved further to the left and "aligned his hope with the world forces that he saw fighting for peace and for the working class."

VIII

For Booker T. Washington, who had been born a slave, the problem of the Negro was to gain acceptance by the white man, especially the Southern white man. He saw education—Negro education—as the solution to this problem. Through education the Negro could acquire the kind of personal virtues and create the kind of community that would win the white man's acceptance. For William E. B. Du Bois, born a free man, it was degrading to seek the white man's acceptance. The black man had a soul, and in America he supposedly had rights, rights that he shared with the white man. The problem of the Negro, therefore, was not to win the white man's acceptance. It was to destroy the white man's discrimination.

Once Du Bois had rejected Washington's approach, one would expect him to reject Washington's faith in the power of education. But the American faith in the power of education is long-abiding. Du Bois, with that naïve snobbery of the intellectual, placed his faith in higher education, reasoning that his fellow white Americans could not deny equal rights to an educated elite, even though they be black. Then seeing his dream of an integrated America shattered against the adamant wall of white prejudice, Du Bois followed his logic into racism, and finally into communism. But those with whom he had shared his dream of an integrated America retained the faith in the power of education. These fellow dreamers focused their hopes on the NAACP. Here education was still the key—once Negroes had a good education then discrimination against them would evaporate. The integrated society would be at hand.

Since the objective was the elimination of white discrimination, the NAACP inevitably adopted the approach of legalism. And since the key to integration was education, the major legal battles against discrimination were all attempts to secure educational opportunities— equal to those given to whites. Finally, since the leaders of the association shared Du Bois' belief in the power of an educated Negro elite to lead the masses in securing their rights, the NAACP directed its legal assaults against discrimination in higher education. Not until the 1950's did the NAACP fight against segregation in the public schools.

In placing its money on the power of an educated elite, the NAACP concerned itself with a minority and showed little worry about the Negro masses. Moreover, in choosing the way of legalism, the NAACP inevitably centered on the Southern states, largely ignoring the increasing numbers of Negroes living in the de facto ghettos of the North. These ghettos in time became infected with all the social ills of the twentieth century. Booker T. Washington's vision of a strong, healthy, Negro community remained a vision, and as the quality and standard of living within the ghettos declined, white fears increased. The fear of contagion reinforced the determination of many whites to keep strong the walls of segregation. Thus, at the very period the NAACP was winning legal victories for the Negro, white prejudice against the Negro was mounting. And as these legal victories became more spectacular, the danger of Negro disenchantment increased—disenchantment that could, and did, lead to despair and finally to violence.

May 17, 1954, was heralded—at the time—as the day

the walls came tumbling down. On that day a unanimous Supreme Court declared, in the case of *Brown v. Topeka Board of Education*, that segregated public schools were unconstitutional. White Southerners greeted the decision with shock, some with fury. The *Washington Post* labeled May 17th as "Black Monday." Negroes, expectedly, hailed the decision with jubilation. True, the actual desegregation of the public schools in the South would have to await a further order of the Supreme Court, which was not to come for another whole year. However, the great day was at hand, the integrated society was here— or soon would be.

The following year, in May 1955, the Supreme Court ordered the racial desegregation of all public schools "with all deliberate speed." However, when the schools opened in September for a new school year nothing happened. Segregation in the South continued as if the Court had never spoken. Confusion and disenchantment rose among Negroes. In December of that year these feelings gathered momentum and found expression in Montgomery, Alabama, setting off what Louis Lomax called the "Negro Revolt."

In that Montgomery bus strike the American Negroes found a new national leader in the Reverend Martin Luther King. Here was the first Negro leader to reject schooling as the panacea for the problem of the Negro. Discrimination continued to be the problem, but the weapon was different. Nonviolent demonstrations were mounted against white discrimination. Yet, although he expressed no great faith in the power of the schools, Martin Luther King did bear witness to the power of education. In point of fact, the whole nonviolent movement was an experiment in educating, an attempt to educate the white man about the extent of discrimination existing in America and to reveal it as a moral evil. Even the Reverend King's claim for "the redemptive power of unmerited suffering," when stripped of its religious connotations is revealed as an educational slogan.

But not all American Negroes followed the lead of Martin Luther King. He had abandoned the unlimited faith in Negro schooling for a belief in the education of the "minds and hearts" of white Americans. Once "educated," these white Americans would help usher in a truly integrated society. Not so, said some. Integration, they declared, will never come. These Black Nationalists urged that Negroes accept, indeed welcome, a segregated America. Rather than beg the white man for an integrated society on his terms, the energies of the blacks should be directed to securing a strong, vigorous, healthy Negro community. Here was a pursuit not unlike that of Booker T. Washington, but lacking his expected payoff of integration into the larger American society. Here too was an educational task. The creation of a strong, vigorous, healthy community required schooling. But the Black Nationalists rejected the schools—the white man's schools—in favor of various informal educational agencies within the ghettos.

Finally there were other Negro leaders in the sixties, such as A. Philip Randolph and James Farmer, who had a different but equally novel vision of the future of American society. Like Washington these leaders wanted an integrated society, but they rejected merit as a prerequisite for integration. From these leaders came demands for job quotas, for preferential hiring of Negroes, for preferential admission to educational institutions, for special or compensatory educational programs, and demands for racially balanced schools. These leaders and their followers were interested in results; they wanted an integrated society; and they wanted it immediately. No longer could they, nor would they, wait for the white community to decide that the Negro merited full admission into American life.

Convinced that the schools were not *the* agency of change, most Negro leaders saw the school as one of the many institutions in American society that needed to be changed, for they realized that instead of integrating black and white children, the schools now actually reinforced the patterns of segregation. In the South "tokenism" in the schools had thwarted the legalistic approach to integration. By admitting a few, selected, compliant Negro pupils to an all-white school while keeping all other Negro children in their "own" schools, Southern communities could comply with the law prohibiting segregated schools. Twelve years after the Brown decision, less than 10 percent of the Negro school children in the South attended schools with whites. So through a "token" compliance with the law, many Southern communities actually used the "desegregated" schools to stymie integration.

In other sections of the country discrimination in housing had created racially segregated residential areas. The children living in these black ghettos attended neighborhood schools within the ghettos. In these de facto segregated schools the Negro children inevitably received an education inferior to that provided in what the Negroes now derided as the "lily-white" schools. What frustrated many Negroes was the fact that attempts to break through the barrier of segregation frequently turned the school systems into a battleground that accelerated racial tensions and intensified segregation. As the Negroes became more militant and more successful in penetrating into the heretofore all-white schools, a tipping point was reached that drove white families out of the community to someplace where the racial balance in the schools was more to their liking. Sometimes white parents removed their children from the public schools and put them into private schools. In some instances the white parents stayed in the community and kept their children in the "racially balanced" schools. But here, more often than not, the schools underwent some significant changes, the principal one usually being the introduction of a "multitrack" system. This system separates children into groups on the basis of what is called "learning ability," which, in effect, separates the children along racial lines. Thus, an ostensibly integrated school on closer examination often proved to be a "cover-up" of a highly segregated educational program.

Yet by the mid-sixties some Negro leaders had second thoughts about integrated schools. By then it was clear that mixing together lower-class Negroes with middle-class whites in the schoolroom did not hasten the day of the integrated society. In those schools that had created a racial balance, the results showed that the lower-class Negro students were not stimulated by being in classrooms with middle-class white children of high aspirations. In fact, as Charles Silberman has pointed out, the Negro students "seemed to give up trying at all." For the white children the integrated classroom created derogatory racial stereotypes, when there had been none before. The children discovered that the Negro children in their classes were "not as bright, clean, honest, or well behaved as they."

In the light of these results some Negro leaders saw that rather than integrated schools, what was *presently* needed was compensatory education for the children in the Negro schools. Only after his schooling placed him on a level with the white child could both profit from an integrated school. Only then would integrated schools lead to an integrated society. Compensatory education for Negro children meant prekindergarten instruction as well as supplemental aid and attention throughout their entire school careers.

Once again the schools were called upon to usher in the integrated society. Would they fulfill the promise this time? History had made one thing clear: since emancipation the school had played a central role in the dreams and the frustrations of the American Negro. While holding out the promise of an integrated society, the American schools had in fact functioned as a barrier against it.

THREE ‖ THE CITY

AND THE

SCHOOLS

I

In 1860 when there were 31 million
people in the United States less than one fifth lived in
cities. Fifty years later the population had increased to
92 million and by then well over two fifths lived in cities.
During this fifty-year period New York City increased
its population fourfold to approach a total of 5 million.
The population of Philadelphia tripled during the same
period, reaching a million and a half by 1910. Chicago,
"the wonder of the West," boasted over 2 million inhabitants in 1910. And in that year St. Louis, Detroit,
Cleveland, and Baltimore each claimed a half million
or more. America was rapidly becoming an urban society.

Most of these urban dwellers were newcomers. Displaced by the ever-increasing mechanization of agricul-

ture, many farmers and sons of farmers came to the city in search of the wealth, the prestige, and the new life styles obtainable through the industrial and commercial jobs that the city now offered. The lure of the city drained the countryside so that by 1890 over 40 percent of the nation's rural townships showed a drop in population.

The shift from the farm to the city was not limited to America. The same forces of mechanization on the farm and improved transportation displaced the agricultural workers in the Old World. But not all European cities could absorb the dislocated farmers. In the cities of Germany and Scandinavia rapid industrialization did create new employment for those displaced from the land. And in Great Britain many erstwhile farmers were diverted to the dominions and colonies—to Canada, to Australia, and to South Africa. But in other nations, especially those in southern and eastern Europe, emigration held the only solution to the problem of rural displacement— emigration to the United States. The exodus to America of displaced farmers from Austria-Hungary, from Italy, and from other southern and eastern European countries was augmented by the addition of thousands of Jews who fled from persecution in Russia during the last quarter of the nineteenth century.

Originally, these "new immigrants" moved west with the frontier, following the path taken by those who had emigrated to America before the Civil War. The railroad companies, anxious to settle the West with potential customers, sent agents to Europe. There they assembled, organized, and herded the immigrants from their native homes all the way to Kansas, or Idaho, or Nebraska. But during the 1880's the westward movement halted. By then the unsold farm lands were beginning to disappear, and cheap land was almost gone. Simultaneously the farmers' income had dropped to a new low, which further dissuaded newcomers from taking up the plow. The new immigrants now sought a livelihood in the mines, in the mills, and in the factories that had mushroomed throughout America during and since the war. It was to the cities that the immigrants now came.

More than five sixths of the Russian-born immigrants —mostly Jews—settled in urban communities. Three quarters of the immigrants from Italy and Hungary congregated in the cities. There, these "new immigrants" joined and were joined by the Irish, who, as Mawdlyn Jones has noted, "from the earliest had showed a marked aversion to a rural existence in America." By 1890 a fourth of the people of Philadelphia and a third of the Bostonians were of alien birth. In greater New York in 1900 four out of five residents were foreign born, or of foreign parentage. In Chicago, the foreign-born exceeded the city's total population of a decade earlier. By 1910 there were well over nine and one-half million foreign born in American cities, together with over twelve million natives of foreign or mixed parentage.

II

The move to the city created problems for the emigrant family. On the farm, or in the village, the family was integrated. Each member had a job, or specific tasks. The entire family, which usually included an aunt or an uncle, as well as some cousins, functioned as an economic unit. Now, in the city, that unity of the family disappeared. In the city the individual, not the family, was the economic unit. The father, usually the older children, and frequently the mother worked outside the home. They worked for an unknown employer, together with unfriendly, impersonal people at some strange, unfamiliar job that lacked meaning because it seemed totally unconnected with the work of anyone else.

Under these conditions the extended family could not hold together. The responsibilities and the duties of the uncles and aunts, of the cousins and the nephews, lacked clear definitions in this new environment. Gradually the family was reduced to parents and their children. And the city transformed them too. On the farm the father had been the head of the household enterprise, but now, in the city, he usually was not the sole, nor sometimes even the main, provider. When employed, he often worked at some menial task that degraded him in his own and his family's eyes. Nor were the women spared. The move to the city upset their routines, changed their roles. The daily tasks required to tend a family and supply its needs seemed infinitely more complex and confusing than on the land. Whether through ignorance and poverty, or through neglect, the crowded family quarters were often disorderly, the food poor or poorly prepared.

For these people the rise of the city represented a radical break with the past. Urbanization meant more than moving from the country to the city, from work on the land to work in the factory. Urbanization involved basic changes in thinking and behavior as well as changes in social values. The migration, the change in occupation, the shifting of status and roles all inflicted substantial damage on the newcomer. Shorn of the shelter of familiar institutions, he suffered a loss of identity. Unprotected and isolated, he became prone to personal deterioration. High rates of mortality, suicide, alcoholism, and insanity showed that, in Oscar Handlin's words, "men raised in one environment could not safely shift to another without substantial damage to themselves."

Yet the decay of traditional institutions was at the same time a release from traditional restraints. To be unsheltered was at the same time to be liberated. So where some succumbed as victims of the city, many newcomers triumphed for the very reasons others failed: the city offered freedom, the opportunity to grow. Many, but not all, grew in the hard testing-ground of the city. To them the slums, the grinding competition, the junglelike complexity, constituted a challenge, not a defeat. And in this race to succeed, the children had a built-in advantage. Born in the city, or brought there as infants, the younger children never experienced the bonds of a pre-urban existence. And for the older children the move to the city signaled the release from traditional restraints. To the children then, if not always to the parents, America, urban America, was the promised land. Instead of the normlessness their parents felt, the children discovered new norms, new *urban* patterns of behavior; instead of alienation, the children developed new attachments in and to the city, uncovered new meanings in the urban way of life; instead of the powerlessness their parents felt, the children hacked out new paths to success, new ways to achieve their goals.

The eagerness and ease with which the young people grasped America contrasted dramatically with the fumbling, hesitant steps of the adults. The gap between generations grew to undreamed-of proportions. On the farm, in the village, the parents had been models for the children. But in this strange new environment, how could the parents guide them, how could the parents protect them from the physical, the social, the moral dangers of the city? Uprooted, unprotected, and isolated, the new-comers no longer possessed adequate norms of behavior. The city had shattered the traditional patterns of life routines, the traditional unfolding of life sequences. Unable to fulfill their traditional role as behavioral models for their children, many parents felt that their children were growing up like savages in the city wilderness. Something had to be done. The children had to be trained; they had to be civilized.

III

As the newcomers from rural America and from Europe moved into the cities many middle- and upper-class citizens moved out. This flight of the upper classes was not caused so much by the influx of newcomers as by the industrialization within the city that brought railroad yards, factories, mills, and commercial establishments of all types into or adjacent to what had been quiet, residential neighborhoods. The city became unlivable for the middle and upper classes. Their abandoned houses were soon stocked with new-comers, overstocked, since shrewd realtors cut up the houses into one- or two-room apartments. Not only the houses but the cellars and the stables became residences for the homeless immigrants. In time the supply of homes gave out and new living quarters were constructed, tenements, usually built side by side and back to back so that there was little light or air.

Crowded into the small rooms and dank hallways with inadequate sanitation and almost no ventilation, many fell victim to tuberculosis, typhoid, diphtheria, scarlet fever. Not only disease but drunkenness, crime, and im-morality flourished under such conditions.

Confronted with the deterioration of their cities, many native urban Americans placed the blame on the newcomers. The immigrants had produced the filth, the vermin, the diseases now found in the cities. The moral inadequacies of the newcomers had generated the slums that were now laying waste to urban life. Their great tendency to vagrancy and crime, their undemocratic backgrounds, and their lack of understanding of American institutions made them a menace to the city, if not to the nation itself. The newcomers were intemperate, illiterate and ignorant; they lived in filth and wallowed in corruption. But what was most frightening of all: they were breeding! Their kids were everywhere, especially in the streets, where they not only got into mischief but frequently committed serious crimes. These "street Arabs" should not be in the streets threatening the life, limb, and property of law-abiding citizens. The schoolroom was where these young hoodlums belonged. It was scandalous that many of these "future citizens" could hardly speak English, let alone read or write it. They needed to be civilized and Americanized—"socialized" was the word frequently used. Education was the only means to save American society from the threat posed by the urban masses. The "battle against the slums," as Jacob Riis termed it, "would be fought out, in, and around the public school."

The children of the newcomers were a problem in another way. Many of them entered the labor market where they worked for low wages. By this they either depressed the salaries of all workers, or worse yet, they displaced some adult from a job. Something had to be done. Some said there ought to be a law to keep them out of the ranks of labor. School is where they belonged, and there ought to be a law to keep them in school.

For their own sake and for the good of society the younger generation had to be constrained. The very stability of democratic society depended upon their being adjusted to the American way of life. Such adjustment required a long period of careful training. Therefore, in order to preserve American democracy the city children had to be institutionalized, had to be compelled to attend school.

IV

Before the Civil War most Americans viewed the very idea of compulsory education with alarm. The nineteenth-century American took the doctrine of limited government seriously. He insisted that the state had no right to interfere between parent and child. The parent, alone, had the right to determine what the child should do, including deciding whether or not he attended school. It is true that the staunchest opponents of compulsory education—both before and after the Civil War—were employers who feared the loss of their child laborers. Nevertheless, American opinion was such that only the state of Massachusetts passed a compulsory attendance law before the Civil War. Even this meager law—compulsory school attendance of every child between eight and fourteen for at least twelve weeks each year, six weeks to be consecutive—proved ineffectual. An agent of the State Board of Education observed as late as 1861 that "compulsion should be used with caution and only as a last resort."

Only after the Civil War, when the rise of the cities created fears for the stability of society, do we find any widespread effort to secure effective compulsory education laws. Four years after the passage of the 1874 com-

pulsory education law in New York the state superintendent reported that the law was effectively enforced
in only New York City and Brooklyn. The same urban
character of compulsory education is evident in the first
law of Maryland, which applied only to Baltimore and
populous Allegheny county. In Missouri school attendance was made compulsory from eight to fourteen only
in cities with a population over 500,000.

The city child, especially the child of the newcomers,
had generated both compassion and fear. He was un-
kempt, uncared for, and untutored. He was in need of
help. But he was also a threat, a threat to the workingman, a threat to social customs, mores, and institutions,
a threat to the future of American democracy. Partly
from fear and partly from compassion, thirty-one states
enacted some form of compulsory education law by
1900. These laws soon transformed American urban
education.

V

Compulsory education laws exploded
school enrollments. The number of five- to eighteen-year-
olds enrolled in school rose from six and a half million
in 1870 to fifteen and a half million by 1880; a rise from
57 percent to over 72 percent of the age group. By 1916
the public schools enrolled twenty million pupils. Compulsory education laws not only brought more children
to the schools but kept them there for longer periods of
time: the average length of a school term rose from 132
days in 1870 to 144 days in 1900, reaching 157 by 1915.

One might expect American schools to be buried by
this avalanche of children. Indeed in the cities additional
buildings and even floors of buildings had to be rented

for use as schools. As late as 1888 one heard complaints about these rented facilities which were "unfit" and a "discredit" to the school system. As rapidly as funds could be secured, sites were purchased and proper school buildings erected. And just as the challenge of inundation spawned new school buildings, so it created an educational profession, for once the American people seriously began to provide mass education, the problems of maintaining schools became so complex that educational experts had to be found and hired to run the schools.

Before the Civil War most urban schools were run by politically appointed trustees of each ward or district, who levied school taxes, built and maintained schoolhouses, and hired the teachers. The economic and social inequalities among the various districts within each city made for glaring educational inequalities. Moreover, the way the politicians handled building contracts and hired teachers led to accusations of graft and corruption. Most cities also had a citywide board of education, but these city boards were large, contentious, and inefficient since they were made up of representatives from every ward or district in the ever-growing city. To get politics out of education and to eliminate some of the educational inequalities, many cities abolished the district system and created in its place a small, manageable board of education for the entire city. Chicago abolished its districts as early as 1857; Philadelphia had districts until 1905, when it reduced the city board from 115 to 24. The members of these new, small boards no longer represented a particular section of the city. They were sometimes elected at large by the people as in Boston and St. Louis, sometimes appointed by the mayor as in Chicago and New York, or even, as in Philadelphia, appointed by the courts.

Once the control of urban education had been centralized in the hands of city boards, these representatives of the public turned much of the power over to a new breed of educational expert, the city superintendent. Although professional school administration starts at this point, the city superintendent was actually not a new employe. Both Buffalo, New York and Louisville, Kentucky had city superintendents as early as 1837. But not until the last decades of the century did the city superintendent become an executive instead of a clerk. In 1895 the U.S. Commissioner of Education could report that the city superintendent retained responsibility for the mechanical elements of curatorship, purchasing supplies, keeping records, and supervising construction of buildings, but that his primary role was that of educational expert: he directed the course of study, taught methods of instruction, served as counselor and advisor to the school board, and fashioned and shaped the educational thought of the community.

These combined duties of supervision and administration proved burdensome for many a city superintendent so that he too had to turn many tasks over to a bevy of specialists. To enforce compulsory education laws, he usually appointed an attendance officer who not only apprehended truant children, but frequently directed the taking of the school census. In addition to truant officers the policing of the city required a vast amount of paper work: age certificates, school certificates, working papers, and employment tickets had to be designed, filled in, and issued. To handle the myriad of forms and affidavits the superintendent acquired a number of assistant superintendents, replete with clerical staffs.

Increasingly superintendents became preoccupied with money. Schoolkeeping was becoming big business. For the country as a whole the value of school property rose from $130 million in 1870 to $1,567 million in 1915, and per pupil expenditure rose from $9.17 a year to $32.53. To manage and control the burgeoning finances most city boards insisted upon appointing a business manager. Finally, to supervise the expanding host of personnel the superintendent came to rely upon special supervisors and principals.

The greatest increase in personnel came in the teaching corps which tripled in size during this period, rising from 200,515 in 1870 to 604,301 in 1915. Yet more significant than the mere increase in their numbers was the fact that in the cities teaching became a profession. In the cities "schoolkeepers" became "schoolteachers." Only later did "schoolteachers" become "educators."

VI

Specialization is the essence of professionalization, and teachers first found the opportunity to specialize in the city schools. Long before the Civil War, teachers in the cities had been able to divide their students into separate classes. But one teacher continued to teach all classes, sometimes assisted by ushers who heard recitations, frequently in the same room with the teacher, while the teacher was hearing the recitation of another class. Horace Mann in his seventh annual report to the Massachusetts Board of Education in 1844 complained that the teacher had too many duties. He supposed that the "perfect school" would be one in which a teacher had "charge of but one class, having talent and resources sufficient properly to engage and occupy its attention." Mann insisted that Massachusetts could have "this mode of dividing and classifying scholars in all our large towns"—

were it not for "that *vis inertiae* of the mind which continues in the beaten track because it has not vigor enough to turn aside from it." A few years later John D. Philbrick organized the Quincy school after the model described by Mann in the seventh annual report. This so-called "graded-school plan" soon spread throughout the country, and by the end of the war most cities and large towns had schools of this type.

In the older, ungraded school the teacher had spent much of his time trying to maintain order, hearing the recitations of one group, or class, at a time. In the new graded school the teacher attended to all students at the same time since he had but one class or grade and so could teach all the students the same material at the same time. The power of the graded school to reduce problems of discipline became one of its most attractive features. William Torrey Harris, onetime superintendent of schools in St. Louis (1868–1880) and later U.S. Commissioner of Education (1889–1906), reported that "it was not uncommon for over 100 cases of corporal punishment to take place in one day" in a St. Louis ungraded school containing about 500 pupils. After the introduction of graded schools Harris claimed that discipline cases dropped in two years from 500 cases per week to 3 cases per week. Now, even the weaker sex could, and did, become schoolteachers in the graded schools of the cities. And since women teachers could be hired more cheaply than men, more and more cost-conscious city boards of education speedily adopted the graded school plan.

The graded school stimulated student effort since all students were expected to complete school by the systematic progression through grades. Lack of effort resulted in being "left down" with the next, younger class. The graded school, for the first time, permitted systematic work. Harris saw the graded school "perfecting the habit of moving in concert with others." He insisted that the graded school in the city was "a stronger moral force than the rural school because of its superior training in the social habits [of] . . . regularity, punctuality, orderly, concerted action and self restraint."

The basis of the graded school was teacher specialization. For the first time the schoolmaster could become a teaching specialist, a specialist in teaching the same material to all the pupils of his class or grade. There was a danger of teaching the same material to all, of course, and as early as 1872, E. E. White complained at the NEA convention of "lock step," mechanical education that geared instruction to average students, thus handicapping the bright and the slow learners. This criticism of the graded school was acknowledged by Harris and others, including Charles W. Eliot, president of Harvard University. But the obvious answer to such criticism, as they pointed out, was more specialization. Thus, we find certain teachers with classes composed only of superior students while others taught only slow learners. In some urban schools, teachers became specialists in one subject. This departmentalization usually took place in the high schools, but a number of cities, beginning with San Francisco in 1887, tried it in the elementary schools. In 1904 New York City introduced the departmental plan in 130 elementary schools. The following year a reporter in the NEA *Proceedings* announced that the teachers were unanimously in favor of the plan, adding that "the age of the Jack-of-all-trades has passed in our vocations and professions."

In most urban schools teachers who were specialists soon acquired special classrooms—for music, for drawing, for physical culture, for domestic science, and for manual training. Frequently in the lower schools there were expression rooms, storytelling rooms, and dramatization rooms.

One of the most remarkable urban developments in teacher specialization was the creation of special city schools and classes for exceptional children. In 1869 Boston instituted the first city school for the education of the deaf. By 1916 seventy-one cities maintained similar schools. New York City established the first public city school for the blind in 1909. By 1916 ten cities had created similar schools. Providence became the first school system to provide special training for the backward child when it organized three schools for special discipline and instruction in 1893. Boston in 1899 and Philadelphia in 1901 took steps to segregate the mentally deficient from regular classes. By 1916, some 118 American cities had organized school classes for the segregation and training of retarded children.

Although this instruction of exceptional children was but one of the many different forms of specialization taking place in education, these teachers decided to appropriate the term "special education." At the NEA convention in 1901 the Department of Deaf and Dumb, Blind, and Feeble-Minded renamed itself the Department of Special Education—"relating to children demanding special means of instruction."

VII

The floodtide of children rushing and being pushed into the city schools did more than create the graded school, for if the graded school offered the schoolmaster the opportunity to become a teaching specialist, then he had somehow to learn that specialty. Up until 1860 only twelve state-supported teacher-training institutions, called normal schools, had been established. After the Civil War the cities for the first time began setting up their own normal schools. By 1871 twelve cities had them and by the end of the century just about every city had one.

Most of these city normal schools were high schools where future teachers received both a general education and professional training. In San Francisco such a program led to a separate postgraduate department of the high school for the professional training of teachers. Many of the city school systems eventually followed St. Louis in developing a full-fledged separate school for the training of teachers.

In these urban normal schools future teachers learned the general method of instruction called "object teaching." Imported into the United States in 1861 by Edward Sheldon, superintendent of schools in the city of Oswego, New York, object teaching had first been developed in England by Charles Mayo and his sister Elizabeth. They, in turn, owed their theories to the famous Swiss educator, Pestalozzi.

Pestalozzi had urged the teacher to begin with the experiences of children; their observations, their ideas. Beginning here, the teacher could proceed by means of carefully graded oral instruction to systematic and organized knowledge. In the system developed by the Mayos the textbook was subordinated to oral instruction so that instead of hearing recitations the teacher directed the learning activity by presenting objects to the children and asking them questions about their observations. "What is this?" begins a typical "model" lesson in Elizabeth Mayo's *Manual*. The lesson continues: "A piece of bark. All look at it. Where do we find bark? On trees.

On what part of trees? Look and see. (The teacher brings in a piece of the stem of a tree on which the bark still remains.) On the outside. Repeat together—'Bark is the outer part of the stems of trees.' " And so on until the end of the lesson when the teacher sums up: "Now repeat all you have said. 'Bark is the outside covering of the stems of trees: it is brown: we cannot see through it: it is rough, dull, dry, hard and fibrous.' "

At the Oswego Normal School teachers were taught how to select lesson materials and arrange them, how to frame questions, and how to conduct the learning exercises. Object teaching soon spread rapidly throughout the country, becoming the main fare of most normal schools. Prior to the Civil War American travelers had described the ideas of Pestalozzi in books and reports, but Pestalozzian principles had "remained largely a matter of lectures and books among the initiated few." Now, after the war, when the rapid growth of the graded school freed the urban schoolmaster to teach, object teaching became *the* method of instruction taught to future teachers.

In the nineties the monopoly of Pestalozzi in America was challenged by a fiery band of educational theorists, who called themselves "Herbartians." Disciples of the German philosopher and educator, Johann Friedrich Herbart (1776–1841), these American reformers claimed to have the final answer to the problem of effective instruction. Herbart, they said, provided the basis for a science of education: education henceforth must be grounded in psychology—the science of the mind.

As Herbart saw it, the teacher's job was to cause the growth of ideas in the mind of the child. Since this required conformity to psychological laws, education depended upon the science of psychology. Pestalozzi had stressed sense perception, and his disciples upheld the doctrine of instruction by object lessons. Herbart, on the other hand, argued that rather than sense perception, teachers must attend to apperception, which he took to be a combination of memory and perception. Rather than having pupils see, hear, and handle things, he told teachers to bring their pupils to recognize things and understand them. For this to occur, the pupils had to see the significance, the usefulness, the applicability of what was taught. And this meant that the ideas had to be properly assimilated; they had to be related to the past experience of the pupil. Herbart's disciples worked out the five formal steps in the process of instruction. First the teacher prepared the mind of the child for the ideas about to be presented; then he presented them. In the third step, the teacher had the student associate or assimilate these ideas with older ideas. Then came the fourth step, generalization. The final step was application or exercise in using the acquired knowledge.

In their efforts to spread their gospel, the Herbartians were indefatigable. In 1889 Charles De Garmo published the first American textbook based upon the pedagogy of Herbart, *The Essentials of Method: A Discussion of the Essential Form of Right Methods in Teaching*. During the next ten years ten more books written or translated by Herbart's American disciples appeared. These textbooks rapidly became the mainstay of most normal schools, as they strove to improve the effectiveness of instruction. At the NEA meeting in July 1895, the Herbartians were in such force that they inaugurated the Herbart Society for the Scientific Study of Teaching, with Charles De Garmo as president.

Yet despite the flurry of textbooks, articles, and yearbooks produced by his American disciples, enthusiasm for Herbart in America was short-lived. Before the end of the century speakers critical of his pedagogical ideas began to dominate the programs of the meetings of the Herbart Society. Finally in 1902 the Society itself changed its name to the National Society for the Scientific Study of Education.

VIII

The fall from grace of Herbart and the Herbartians was due to the simple fact that they had too narrow a concept of the role of the teacher. This is evident in the change in name of the society, from "the scientific study of teaching" to "the scientific study of education." The Herbartians failed to see the teacher as an educator at the very moment that urban Americans were rejecting "teachers" in favor of "educators."

Recall that the rise of the city had generated a crisis in the minds of most American adults. Whether they were newcomers or oldtimers, they saw the younger generation growing up in a world they never knew— a different world. To them the children of the city seemed a different species. Many adults felt themselves witness to a kind of degeneration. As the tide of immigration from rural America and from Europe to the teeming cities of the New World rose higher and higher in the first years of the twentieth century, the fears of inundation and nostalgia for the simpler, more civilized past grew apace.

Many now redoubled the demand that the schools combat the ills of urbanization. The stick of compulsory education laws had been taken up to drive the young savages into the schools. These laws had spawned a profession of schoolteachers and a profession of school administrators as well as a science of education. But this was not enough. True, the cities now had better buildings, better trained teachers, and more effective instruction than could be found in rural America. But the improvement of effective instruction seemed to many to be patently ineffective in curing the ills of the city, for, no matter how improved the instruction in the city schools, many students remained uninterested in what was being taught. Many dropped out of school after a year or two. One study made of the schools in St. Louis concluded that the primary cause for pupil withdrawal was "a lack of interest on the part of the pupil"; the second cause was "a lack on the part of the parents of a just appreciation of the education now offered." Obviously the schools could not successfully combat the ills of the city if they could not keep their pupils. Many now began to argue for changes in the content of instruction.

Herbart had not tampered with the traditional curriculum, although he had urged teachers to make that curriculum more meaningful to students. He, himself, for example, had proven to his own satisfaction that the *Odyssey* became more meaningful to his students when taught in Greek, rather than in translation. He never questioned the teaching of the *Odyssey* itself.

At the fourth annual meeting of the Herbart Society in 1898, M. G. Brumbaugh, professor of history from the University of Pennsylvania, decried the narrow outlook of the Herbartians. History, he insisted, "should be so presented as to arouse the social sense of the child." That same year Spencer Trotter of Swarthmore, in a speech entitled "The Social Function of Geography," told the members of the Herbart Society that the end of the study of geography was "to develop a social intelligence and, consequently, a social disposition."

The following year, at the fifth annual meeting, I. W. Howerth delivered a major revisionist talk entitled, "The Social Aims in Education." Reflecting both a holistic and organic conception of society, Howerth warned that the two great dangers of an urbanized society were the atomization of the individual and the retardation of social progress. To prevent these twin evils Howerth insisted that the aim of education should be "The adaptation of the individual to the prosecution and enjoyment of a social life, the elimination of anti social feeling, and the development of sympathetic emotions." In this way education will "modify and accelerate social evolution." For, he pointed out "so long as certain classes or certain individuals refuse to recognize their natural relations to society, so long will they tend to retard the advance of society toward its ultimate goal." Howerth summed up this new aim of education in the term "socialization." He took pains to point out that socialization went beyond, and indeed was unlike, "preparation for social life." The Herbartians themselves admitted "preparation for social life" as an aim of education and argued that Herbart's goal of developing many-sided interests in the child was the best preparation for social life. But for Howerth, rather than preparation for social living, socialization meant "a reorganization of the school so as to give all its activity a social value and in such a way that it will reflect and organize the fundamental principles of community life."

Here at last was a response to assuage the fears and nurse the nostalgia of urban Americans. Here at last was a theory of education that could combat the ills of the city by doing battle with urbanization itself. According to this theory the city schools were to do no less than recapture the community of the remembered past. What appealed to many was that this movement to recapture the past was not reactionary but progressive, since, according to the theory, the progress of society itself necessitated the restoration of community. As the primary agency of socialization the school would restore the community and thereby guarantee the very progress of society.

IX

I. W. Howerth taught at the University of Chicago, and in his talk he had referred generously and respectfully to his colleague, John Dewey, head of the unified Department of Philosophy, Psychology, and Pedagogy. With John Dewey the pleas for restoration of community rested on more than a hankering for the past. Without community, the bigness of the city, its variety, and its toleration shattered the individual, leaving him undisciplined, dislocated, and alienated. But Dewey thought that the restoration of community could transform these same conditions so that they would promote the growth of the individual and the growth of society itself. Here we find the man who first articulated those holistic and organic conceptions of society that uncovered the twin evils of urbanization: individual atomization and social retardation. Here, too, we find the man first to prescribe the restoration of community as the cure for these ills. And it was Dewey who gave this restoration job to the schools.

As early as 1896 Dewey had set up the Laboratory School at the University of Chicago, a school he described as "a cooperative society on a small scale." The expressed aim of his school was the "ability of individuals to live in cooperative integration with others." In the same year that Howerth delivered his address to the Herbart Society, John Dewey published his epoch-making book, *School and Society*. In this book the Vermont-bred philosopher insisted that city youths lacked the educational experiences common in preurban America. Growing up in rural America the child had had a direct contact with reality, hence an understanding of the world in which he lived, a far better understanding than did the city child of the present. On the farm, or in the small village, unlike the city, Dewey wrote, "the entire industrial process stood revealed," from the production on the farm of the raw materials "till the finished product was actually put to use." If the family did not itself produce all the necessities of life then it obtained the flour, the lumber, the wool, from "shops in the immediate neighborhood, shops open to investigation and often the center of neighborhood congregation."

Not only did the rural child have this direct contact with reality, but almost always, Dewey pointed out, he had a share in the work; he had his chores, his duties, his responsibilities. The performance of these necessary tasks built character and developed discipline. The child acquired habits of order and industry, he accepted responsibility, he learned to cooperate with others. But in the city the child had few if any chores or duties, and the nonperformance of them rarely produced dire consequences. The city child did not participate in securing the necessities of life, so whatever chores he had were a burden, a drudgery, something to be avoided. The city child did not learn to cooperate with others, rejected responsibility, and rarely acquired the habits of order and industry. In rural America "the educative forces of the domestic spinning and weaving, of the sawmill, the gristmill, the copper shop and the blacksmith forge were continually operative," Dewey explained. But in the city the child grew up unable to grasp the meaning of the phenomena he encountered daily. The significance of events—of rain, of the change of seasons—escaped him. The logical interconnectedness of things was gone. The complexity of the city had cut the child off from reality, stunted character development, and hindered the growth of cognitive processes. The city had atomized the child.

Now, Dewey argued, the city school had to become a truly educative institution. In the past the school had provided "schooling" while the society itself had "educated" the child, educated him in the very process of his growing up. Since urban society no longer educated, the school must assume this role, must abandon the aim of teaching "set lessons" and strive instead to develop the "spirit of social cooperation and community life."

In the Laboratory School at the University of Chicago, the children engaged in the basic activities, activities that provided man's fundamental needs. In this school the children spent most of their time in play and work activities: gardening, weaving, making things in wood and metals. Through these activities, the children, in effect, grew through or recapitulated the history of man's attempt to secure food, clothing, and shelter. As the child advanced, he discovered "how the sciences gradually grew out from useful occupations: physics out of the use of tools and machines, chemistry out of the professions of dyeing, cooking, metal smelting, etc." In this mode of schooling the child became "familiar with many aspects of knowledge in relation to living." Here the artificiality of the traditional curriculum was overcome by revealing to the child the social uses of knowledge.

By transforming the school into a place where the children engaged in "real life activities," Dewey expected to do more than overcome the alienation of the child from the curriculum. In this school the child engaged in joint activity to solve shared problems. He learned cooperation and self-discipline. This school was a community, and in it the child learned the values of community and how to function together with others in a community. Once the school became a community, then, Dewey insisted, it would serve as a model for the larger society; the school would be "the best guarantee of a larger society which is worthy, lovely and harmonious."

X

In charging the schools with such an awesome responsibility, Dewey had concocted a new role for the teacher. The aim of socialization, to use Howerth's term, meant that henceforth the teacher was to be an educator, not a mere schoolteacher. The job of socializing the young went beyond the adding or dropping of courses and subjects according to their social relevancy. Now, in a most significant sense, the educator "taught children, not subjects." It was at this point that the specialization in teaching, which had flourished in the urban environment, began to peter out. Instead of a specialist responsible for one small segment of the child's education, each teacher now was responsible for the "whole child."

Forged in the face of advancing hordes of pupils brought to the school door by compulsory education laws, specialization—after creating superior urban school systems—was now to be undermined by the theory of socialization. Yet who can deny that this new aim of education had been implicit in the early reactions to the ills of urbanization? To cure these ills Americans had turned to their schools, so if the traditional schooling did not do the job, then, indeed, the schools must be transformed. This transformation of the city schools did not stop with the expansion of the responsibility of the teacher, who now taught, or socialized, the whole child. This transformation soon extended the functions of the school itself. Once again John Dewey helped to show the way.

In 1902 Dewey gave a talk at the NEA convention entitled "The School as a Social Center," in which he pointed out that the schoolhouse must become "a center of full and adequate social service"; it must be brought "completely into the current of social life." In his talk Dewey confined himself to the philosophy of the school as a social center, but he stated that he felt that the philosophical aspect of the matter was not the "urgent" or "important" one. "The pressing thing, the significant thing," he said, "is really to make the school a social center. . . ." A few years later, in 1911, the yearbook of the National Society for the Study of Education enthusiastically presented a composite picture of the transformed American schoolhouse. This yearbook, entitled "The City School as a Community Center," revealed that the schools in city after city had taken on new tasks, new functions. Here one found described the public lecture series in Cleveland, the vacation playgrounds in Newark, the organized athletics in New York, the home and school associations in Philadelphia, and the widely acclaimed Civic and Social Center in Rochester.

The city of Rochester in 1907 had hired Edward Ward to conduct an experiment in the community use of schoolhouses. Ward established social centers that not only contained recreational and industrial training facilities but also served as "a citizens' council chamber," a place in which to develop the citizens' capacity for intelligent government. The social center, in Ward's words, was "just to be the restoration of its true place in social life of that most American of all institutions, the Public School Center, in order that through this extended use of the school building might be developed, in the midst of our complex life, the community interest, the neighborly spirit, the democracy that we knew *before we came to the city.*"

XI

Describing the American city in 1921, Lord Bryce said that the inhabitants "were not members of a community but an aggregation of human atoms, like grains of desert sand, which the wind sweeps hither and thither." The quest for community remained unfulfilled. And so long as the newcomers, themselves uprooted and considered a menace by the natives, continued to pour into the city, the battle against atomization seemed hopeless.

During the first decade of the century over eight and a half million immigrants came to America. Another four million arrived between 1910 and 1914. The First World War practically stopped all immigration. Moreover, the war aroused antialien sentiments along with fears of allegedly unassimilated "hyphenated-Americans." The bitterness and hatred toward the foreign born was more evident among rural Americans, who had little direct contact with the foreigners. These forces were powerful enough, however, to get Congress to pass an immigration restriction law over President Wilson's veto. Four years later the first Immigrant Quota Act passed, and it was followed in 1924 by a second, more restrictive quota system. Actually, immigration had never risen to the million-a-year rate of the prewar years, although by the twenties it rose to well above a half million a year. But after 1924, the Quota Act drastically reduced the numbers coming to America.

Perhaps now the schools could overcome the atomization of urban life. Perhaps now they could recapture the community. But this, of course, did not happen. Within a few years the city schools confronted a new problem, a catastrophe that displaced all earlier anxieties about the ills of urbanization. In the thirties, the American school took on one of its most awesome responsibilities: the Depression. The Depression of the thirties was the worst in American history. More than an economic crisis this disaster all but shattered the abiding American faith in social progress. Could the schools restore that faith? Some argued that the schools not only could, but that they must go even further and create a new social order. The schools, these people argued, must reconstruct society itself.

The Depression further reduced migration to the city, from home and abroad, so urbanization did diminish as a problem during this period. More to the point, however, is the fact that the ills caused by the Depression cut across all geographic lines. The traditional distinctions between urban problems and rural problems were lost in the suffering shared by all. So it happened that people stopped talking about city schools and rural schools. American educators now talked in terms of *the American* school and its role in American society.

Concerned more with social progress and less with human atomization, schoolmen now needed a school different from Dewey's Laboratory School, different from Ward's social centers. They called their new kind of school the "community school." In this school, improvement of the community or improvement of community living became the primary function. The carrying out of this function required more than infusing school children with the "spirit of social cooperation and community life," as Dewey had tried to do in the Chicago Laboratory School. And it required more than transforming the school into a place for communal activities as Ward had done in Rochester. Unlike their predecessors in the first decades of the century, those in the thirties who spoke about this new community school assumed that the community existed. With them the quest for community gave way to requests for community service.

First of all, according to its advocates, the community school accepted the total community as the educative agency. Following Dewey they distinguished "schooling" from "education" and opted for the latter. Dewey, in his Laboratory School, had tried to substitute "education" for "schooling" by transforming the school into an "embryonic community active with types of occupations that reflect the life of the larger society." But these new educators of the thirties abandoned the attempt to turn the school into a community. They said education must take place through actual participation in the larger society itself. The students in a community school discovered that the walls were down. They went outside the school to study the needs and problems of their own community. In fact, they made proposals to meet the needs and solve the problems they found. Students engaged in these "worthwhile projects" made surveys of the local industries, stores and markets; they investigated the educational facilities, the public welfare agencies, the recreational opportunities, and the public utilities; they probed the systems of transportation and communication. The government itself came under their scrutiny, as did the local customs, mores, and peculiarities. Once they identified the problems and ascertained the needs, the students made recommendations.

In Flint, Michigan, for example, the students made a traffic survey and devised a safety program. They also made a housing survey, exploring the matters of home-ownership and population density. Emily R. Kickhafer, supervisor of social studies in the Flint public schools, supplied the students with a questionnaire to facilitate the analysis. The questionnaire contained questions like: "What can a local community do to guide housing?" "How may public opinion toward building be molded?" "How is it going to be possible to get out of the jam in which housing finds itself?"

The concept of the total community as the educative agency, in addition to implying that the students could and should be educated through "projects" in the community, also implied that all members of the community were educators. In other words, just as the school no longer was the sole agency of instruction, so the teacher was no longer the sole educator. Convinced that "adults and children have common purposes," the directors of the community schools secured the cooperation of the adults in the community, who then actively participated in these projects in cooperation with the children. When, in 1938, Paul Misner, director of community education, drew up a program of "areas of experience" for the entire educational system of Glencoe, Illinois, he included planned, cooperative experiences for pupils and adults throughout the entire program. At the primary levels (ages six to eight) parents and lay citizens cooperated in taking excursions to farms, dairies, the post office, the telegraph office, the railway station, the fire house, the police station, and stores. In addition Misner scheduled "cooperative activities in which adults and children plan teas, bird sanctuaries, community programs, etc." At the secondary level adults cooperated in a variety of projects, including studies of municipal government "to determine how it can best serve the needs of the community." In this program of planned "areas of experience" adult involvement continued through the college years.

It was the hope of the directors of the community schools that through participation in these projects the youth would develop into citizens who would participate intelligently and efficiently in community enterprises. In this way the growth and development of all members of the community would lead directly to the improvement of the community itself.

Educators continued to endorse the community school after the Second World War and on into the fifties. In 1953 the National Society for the Study of Education (NSSE) devoted its yearbook to the topic "The Community School." But by the fifties, as the articles in the yearbook reveal, the message had begun to pale; the proposals now sounded like the slogans of an era long past. In 1953 it was strange to hear an educator say that "the role of education is seen to be more than intellectual training." In the fifties it no longer seemed fitting to regard the school "as an agency for helping to give direction to community growth and development."

Already dissatisfied with the schools, parents were in no mood to tolerate these notions of the so-called "community school." American education was undergoing a "searching reappraisal." In 1953, the same year of the fifty-second NSSE yearbook, a rash of books appeared that pungently criticized the teachers, the schools, and the entire system. The titles reveal both the tone and the thrust: *Quackery in the Public Schools, Educational*

Wastelands, The Conflict in Education, Let's Talk Sense About Our Schools.

Arthur Bestor, a history professor, who wrote *Educational Wastelands,* lambasted the "educators," making the term one of contempt. "The school makes itself ridiculous," he wrote, "whenever it undertakes to deal directly with 'real life problems' instead of indirectly through the development of generalized intellectual powers." He insisted that "genuine education" is "intellectual training." Many agreed. And who could take "educators" who endorsed the community schools seriously after Bestor reminded everyone that "the men who drafted our constitution were not trained for the task by 'field trips' to the mayor's office and the county jail."

Before the decade ended, the community school had been ridiculed out of existence. When intellectuals had complained about American schools in the thirties, no one had listened. But by the fifties the intellectual in America had come to enjoy more acceptance. Now, according to Richard Hofstadter, the life of the intellect "took on a more and more positive meaning." The leaders of business, of government, of the military all discovered a need for the services of the intellectual, the expert. The Russian sputnik in 1957 merely reinforced this need. And the community school? Had it improved community living throughout America? Probably no more than the predepression urban schools had succeeded in their quest to restore the village community.

XII

In the sixties Americans once again distinguished urban education from the rest of American education. Urban education, and the problems of education in the city, now seemed worthy of special attention. But by the sixties most educators had abandoned the quest for community; most had given up the notion that the primary function of the urban school was to combat urbanization. Now most accepted urbanization as a fact of twentieth-century life. The community had been eclipsed. Educators, lacking both a memory and a dream of a stable society, were less and less concerned with socialization.

Like their colleagues at the turn of the century, the urban educators of the sixties took their pedagogical cues from parents. And by this time the dispersal of political power in urban America had given voice to parents who were hip. They did not seek the restoration of a community few of them had ever known. They might not themselves be models of what they wanted their children to become, but they knew what was needed to make good. And to make good meant to break out of the city. The city for the majority of its inhabitants was no longer the promised land. The city had become the land of bondage. The schools offered a way out. This deterioration of the city can be explained largely in terms of the patterns of mobility that formed in the forties and fifties.

Residential mobility played a significant role in this pattern. After both the Second World War and the Korean conflict, the largess of the federal government provided veterans with no-money-down mortgages that allowed many city dwellers to purchase the home they had never dared to dream of before. Moreover, the general wave of prosperity during and after the war prompted many other city families to buy a home of their own. The housing boom created to meet this demand took place outside the city where the land cost less and the building restrictions were more relaxed.

Not all city dwellers moved to the suburbs. But not all of those who remained in the city did so voluntarily. Racial discrimination kept the nonwhite family—ex-GI or not—out of the suburbs. At the same time a widening stream of Southern Negroes poured into the Northern cities. In New York City, for example, the special census of 1957 revealed an increase since 1950 of some 320,000 nonwhites. This increase, together with a decrease of some 416,000 whites, greatly raised the percentage of nonwhites living within the city. In the decade 1950–1960 New York City lost about 1,300,000 middle-class whites, a number exceeding the population of Cleveland, Ohio. It gained 800,000 Negroes and Puerto Ricans. New York's population shift was more dramatic than that of any other city, but it was typical of what occurred in other major cities during this period. By 1960, 75 percent of the Negroes in the United States were urban dwellers. Outside the South, over 90 percent lived in cities.

In all cities discriminatory housing restrictions forced the nonwhite population to remain within the walls of their ghettos, and the congestion brought on by these restrictions caused the rapid deterioration of living conditions within the ghetto. Expectedly, there was a decline in civic mindedness, a loss of civic conscience. Moreover, the apathy, the ineptitude, and the inaction of city governments reinforced the diminished civic mindedness of the nonwhites. The city fathers now took their cues from the whites remaining within the city. These were the very rich and the very poor, the very old and the not very ambitious. To all of them—either because they had so much to lose, or because they had so little—change was a threat. They all viewed the rumblings within the ghetto with fear and anger. The political moves made by city governments inevitably reflected these emotions.

In some cases the city fathers did try to do something constructive to prevent the rumbling ghetto from exploding. But municipal efforts at urban renewal, hampered by insufficient funds, proved inadequate. Part of the financial plight of the cities, of course, was due to the flight to the suburbs. Once he located in suburbs, the new homeowner began to spend his money there. Stores and shops in the cities closed down and moved to the greener fields outside the city limits. And when the city fathers tried to recoup their lost revenue by raising taxes on real estate, or by levying a sales tax, they only made matters worse, for rather than pay the increased taxes, more people fled from the city. As a result properties within the city fell into the hands of speculators, who, to avoid tax hikes, allowed the property to deteriorate while they increased their own revenue by raising the rent—or the number of tenants. Gradually the city succumbed to what was called urban blight.

Most analyses of the decline of the city attribute importance to the postwar patterns of occupational mobility as well as to the patterns of residential mobility. During this period the traditional patterns of occupational mobility disappeared.

Traditionally newcomers to the city began on the lowest rung of the occupational ladder, as unskilled workers. Then in different ways, and with varying degrees of success, they worked their way up that ladder. Some did it by becoming entrepreneurs, usually catering to the specific needs and wants of their own group. Often they succeeded, following the traditional pattern from pushcart vender to grocer, to wholesaler or distributor, or from skilled worker to subcontractor, to manufacturer. Sometimes the newcomer remained in an unskilled or semiskilled job his entire working life, projecting his hopes and aspirations into his children. For them he worked, scrimped, and saved so that they could go to school and advance up the occupational ladder into clerical, managerial, even professional positions.

In the forties and fifties the principal newcomers to the cities came from the Western Hemisphere, not from Europe. As mentioned above, thousands of Negroes from the South and Puerto Ricans settled in the northeastern cities—in Philadelphia, in Newark, in New York. Southern Negroes and Appalachian whites migrated to the cities of the Midwest—to Detroit, to Cincinnati, to Cleveland, to Chicago. Negroes, Mexican-Americans, and reservation Indians flocked to Western cities—to Los Angeles, to Oakland, to Phoenix.

These newcomers shared one thing with earlier migrants to the city—they were desperately poor. But they soon found that the traditional path of occupational mobility used by their predecessors was closed to them.

On the one hand, bigness had squelched entrepreneurship as a way of rising. Supermarkets, department stores, discount houses, chain stores, suburban shopping centers —all made it difficult, if not impossible, for the poor newcomer to start out in business for himself. And the father who tried to stick to his unskilled job in order to send his children to school soon discovered that he was expendable; his work could better be done by a machine. Nor could he easily find a semiskilled job since most of the large manufacturing plants had moved out of the cities. The poor city dweller found himself cut off from these jobs because the inadequacies, or the high cost, of public transportation prohibited him from commuting from his home to the plant.

The loss of job opportunities within the city forced many to "go on welfare." This enforced idleness frequently sapped all initiative from the workingman, and the spectacle had a deleterious impact on the aspirations of the young. Why bother trying if you cannot get a job? Often the city youth, particularly if a Negro, already suffered from the absence of a father in the home—someone to imitate, to prove oneself to, perhaps to fight against. The Negro youth in the city frequently lacked someone to encourage his efforts, to applaud his triumphs; he had no one to protect him or solace him when he failed. As a result, often the Negro youth drew back from trying.

Technological change, uninhibited technological change, had reduced job opportunities for newcomers to the city. James B. Conant commented in a study in the early sixties that in the slum area of a large city containing 125,000 people, mostly Negro, roughly 70 percent of the boys and girls aged sixteen to twenty-one were out of school and unemployed. Throughout the nation in 1961 only 50 percent of Negro men (compared with two-thirds of white men) worked steadily at full-time jobs. By 1963, although Negroes comprised only 10 percent of the labor force, they accounted for 20 percent of total unemployment, and nearly 30 percent of long-term unemployment, that is, unemployment lasting twenty-seven weeks or longer.

In the sixties no one denied the fact that all cities contained great numbers of unemployed nonwhites. But there was deep disagreement about the significance of this massive unemployment. Many whites took this to mean that the Negro had no desire to work; he had come to the city in order to get the welfare benefits available there. If the Negro really wanted to work, the argument went, he would get up and get a job; he lacked initiative and wanted something for nothing.

This demeaning interpretation of Negro unemployment, rarely openly voiced by public officials, nor expressed in the press, was nonetheless widespread among all classes of whites, urban and nonurban as well. This white man's interpretation, usually snidely implied, infuriated the urban Negro. As he saw it, the widespread unemployment was due to racial discrimination. Negroes and Puerto Ricans, Mexicans and Indians just never were hired or promoted to certain jobs. Some commentators have called this the concept of "place." Often an unconscious prejudice on the part of those who hired and promoted kept minority groups out of the better jobs; it also destroyed their aspirations for those jobs.

The urban Negro, convinced that it was the white man's prejudice that kept him out of work, found himself pushed to the breaking point when taunted by the same white man's accusations of laziness and lack of initiative. This was the "social dynamite" that exploded in major cities during the decade of the sixties when racial riots amounting almost to insurrections rocked New York City, Rochester, Cleveland, Chicago, and, worst of all, Los Angeles and Detroit.

By the mid-sixties the federal government and many state governments had laws prohibiting discriminatory hiring practices. The machinery to administer these laws often remained weak, but Negroes and other minority groups now began to penetrate into new occupations, especially government jobs and jobs with firms that catered to mass consumers. But the passage of these fair employment laws had a dramatic impact on the interpretations and understanding of the patterns of occupational mobility. Now many came to the conclusion that the crucial obstacle to Negro employment and occupational mobility was neither white racial discrimination, nor Negro lack of initiative. Attempts to implement these fair employment practices revealed that the years of discrimination had taken their toll. Not expecting ever to get more than a menial job, Negro youths had not prepared themselves for entry into "white man's occupations." Time and time again stories were told of firms who found it impossible to find qualified Negroes to fill better jobs. Negro youths were unprepared, unqualified, and unready for these jobs. Here was a new obstacle to occupational mobility.

The American answer to this problem, obviously, was education. The schools would prepare Negroes for the better, available jobs. The schools would qualify them for movement up the occupational ladder, ready them for entry into what was once the white man's world of work. In the sixties the urban schoolmasters heeded this cry for career preparation. The more ambitious parents demanded that the schools, from kindergarten through high school, prepare *their* children for admission to college. The less ambitious insisted that the schools teach *their* children some marketable skills.

The new concern with the occupational power of schooling let loose a flood of troubles for urban educators. Negroes, and members of other minority groups, complained loudly and angrily about the unequal educational provisions they had previously accepted. These parents pointed out that the schools that served their children had the oldest, most dilapidated equipment and facilities, the most incompetent teachers, the most watered down, irrelevant educational programs.

Urban educators responded with projects and programs that stressed academic studies and emphasized vocational preparation. At a 1962 federal conference on "The Impact of Urbanization on Education" those attending concluded that "Every teacher, then, is in essence a vocational educator." In line with this career orientation urban educators spent considerable time, energy, and money on programs of counseling and guidance.

Once the city schools had narrowed their function to instruction in academic and vocational subjects, much attention focused on the matter of the efficiency and efficacy of that instruction. This produced the so-called "revolution in teaching," a revolution in instructional techniques. In the perspective of history this was almost a "missed revolution." Some sixty years earlier, as we saw, the demands for socialization had undermined the advances made in the urban schools' instructional practices. Those advances had resulted from the increased specialization in the city schools. The revolution in teaching of the sixties signaled a return to specialization.

Schools of education now could not keep up with the urban school systems' demands for more and more specialists. Reading, art, and music specialists became commonplace in the urban elementary schools. In addition to the expansion of subject matter specialization, there were specialists in types of pupils: teachers of disturbed children; teachers of culturally deprived or slum children; teachers of fast learners and of slow learners. In the sixties educators only started to tap the infinite varieties of special education that could be used to improve instruction. During this decade they came to realize that the path to instructional improvement led to a diminution in scope of the duties of the individual teacher.

During this period teachers ceased trying to be psychologist-sociologist-group worker-counselor-therapist to his students. Specialists took over these jobs, and the teacher taught mathematics, or whatever his specialty was.

Throughout the twentieth century the urban school had played a role in both occupational and residential mobility—the more highly educated urbanites moved up the occupational ladder and out of the city. Despite all the nostalgic and romantic notions about the community voiced over the years by urban pedagogues, the urban school had in fact functioned as an escape hatch from the city. Finally, in the sixties, Americans explicitly recognized this function.

FOUR || ECONOMIC
OPPORTUNITY
AND THE
SCHOOLS

I

From the beginning Americans called
their country the "land of opportunity." In America,
Crèvecoeur reported in 1782, "one does not find, as in
Europe, a crowded society, where every place is overstocked. There is room for everybody in America. Has
he any particular talent or industry? He exerts it in order
to procure a livelihood, and it succeeds."

Americans had little cause to doubt that America indeed was the land of opportunity until after the Civil
War. In 1873, following a few years of jubilant postwar
prosperity, the country entered a depression that lasted
for six long years. There had been depressions before,
but none like this. Depressions hit industrialized nations
much harder than agricultural ones. Industrialization had

mushroomed in America during and after the war so that the depression of the seventies took a deadly toll.

Three million workers faced unemployment, one fifth of the working class. Another two fifths worked but six to seven months a year. In New York City a quarter of the total labor force was out of work. According to Henry Pelling, "no other depression in American history, except that of the 1930's, was so severe." Only one-fifth of the working class retained regular employment throughout the six-year period. In the fall of 1877, the low point of the depression, one New York worker rhetorically asked: "What are the carpenters doing? Nothing! What are the bricklayers doing? Nothing! What do they have to live on this coming winter? Nothing!"

Yet at the very moment the hopes of the many were fading, the fortunes of a few were soaring. Even before the depression, the progress of industrialization had been marked by the combination of businesses into bigger units. In 1870 the son of an itinerant medicine seller organized the Standard Oil Company of Ohio. Within eight years Standard Oil controlled 95 percent of the pipe lines and refineries in the United States. The thirty-eight-year-old John D. Rockefeller was well on his way to becoming "the most feared and hated man in America." Yet only later in the eighties did the public gain knowledge of the vast holdings of Rockefeller and the tactics of oppression, extortion, and price controls used by Standard Oil.

During the depression, the most widely known man of wealth was the rough-and-ready Commodore Vanderbilt. In 1855 Vanderbilt had been listed as merely one of nineteen New Yorkers whose wealth was estimated at more than a million dollars. By the end of the war he was the only American worth more than $20 million. Vanderbilt amassed his millions by keeping up with the technological revolution going on in transportation. Starting with a dilapidated ferry, the Commodore built a fleet of river steamboats. Then, moving from the waterways to the rails, he became the railroad king of the seventies. He died in January 1877, leaving an estate of $105 million. For a boy born in the one-room cabin of a ferryboat worker, Vanderbilt had done well, very well indeed! Here was proof that America was still the land of opportunity. Or was it?

Four months after the revelation of the Commodore's legacy, the railroad workmen read that their wages were being cut because the railroads were in trouble. The first announcement of a wage cut came from the New York Central, the line owned by the Vanderbilts. All the other lines followed. Opportunity, apparently, was limited to the few and denied to the many. On July 17, the day after the wage cut went into effect, the United States had its first major railroad strike. Starting on the Baltimore & Ohio line in West Virginia, it spread north to Canada and west to California. Frightened governors across the land called their militia. Railroad cars were burned; rifles and Gatling guns began going off. Violence flared in West Virginia, in Maryland, in New York, in Illinois, in Pennsylvania. A pitched battle between the strikers and militia reached the level of an insurrection in Pittsburgh. There, after killing twenty-six, and wounding hundreds more, the militia retreated in the face of a wild, incendiary mob. For a day and a half law and order disappeared as the riotous mob proceeded to burn, loot, and destroy. When it had spent itself, the mob had destroyed over $5 million worth of railroad property. But the wage cut remained intact.

While the workers slunk back to work, a shocked nation wondered where it would all lead. One historian, James Rhodes, who had lived through the strike, later wrote, "We had hugged the delusion that such social uprisings belonged to Europe and had no reason of being in a republic where there was plenty of room and an equal chance for all." People wondered, Was America still the land of opportunity? More and more Americans began to feel that opportunity had all but disappeared from the land. And always someone appeared who would fan this discontent, like Henry George, a San Francisco newspaperman who wrote a book called *Progress and Poverty*. In it he argued that the progress of the few had been built on the poverty of the many. George's solution to eliminating the gap between the rich and the poor consisted of a plan for a single tax, a tax on land. Other reformers made different proposals, some more, some less radical than that proposed by George.

The ending of the depression in 1879 quelled much of the uneasiness, but the lesson of those hard times remained. If the workingmen of America were to lose their belief that theirs was the land of opportunity, this could open the door to radicalism and violence. At least this was how it looked from the top. The wealthy were getting frightened; to assuage their fears, the faith of the workingman must be restored. And the workingman, ready and anxious to reaffirm his belief in America, avidly clutched at the words of those who told him there was room at the top.

II

Success literature was not unknown in America. One of the earliest—and most famous—"success manuals" had been compiled in 1757 by Benjamin Franklin under the title "The Way to Wealth." Others had written similar handbooks since the days of Franklin. But never had there appeared so many books "pointing out the high road to prosperity." Printing houses now turned them out by the thousands. Irwin Wylie has estimated that of all the success manuals published before the year 1900, four out of five appeared after the Civil War. And more were published between 1880 and 1885 than in any other five-year period.

In 1882, P. T. Barnum published *The Art of Money Getting*, followed by *How I Made Millions* (1884). The founder of the Mellon banking fortune published his autobiography in 1885, *Thomas Mellon and His Times.* In 1887 Henry Clews published his memoirs, *Twenty Years on Wall Street.* But most of the millionaires had neither the time nor the talent to write their own biographies. Journalists supplied the bulk of biographical data on the rich men of America. James Parton published a collection of biographies of millionaires in a two-volume work in 1884. He called it *Captains of Industry.* Other biographical accounts appeared in *Room at the Top,* edited by Adam Craig in 1883.

In addition to serving as the subjects for biographies most millionaires willingly gave interviews and responded to questionnaires. A large number of books based on such materials appeared in the eighties: William S. Speer, *The Law of Success* (1885); Wilbur F. Crofts, *Successful Men of Today and What They Say of Success* (1883); Francis E. Clark, *Our Business Boys* (1884). Clark, a clergyman, published a second book publicizing the secrets of success in 1885; he called it *Danger Signals, The Enemies of Youth from the Business Man's Standpoint.* Another clergyman, Lyman Abbott, wrote

How to Succeed (1882). Nelson Sizer published *The Royal Road to Wealth* in 1882, followed by *The Road to Success* in 1884. Many books had similar titles. People sometimes confused Edwin T. Friendly's *The Secret of Success in Life* (1881) with William Farrar's *Success in Life* (1885). The prolific William Makepeace Thayer, who later edited a magazine simply called *Success*, gave one of his books the snappy title *Tact, Push, and Principle* (1881).

What were the secrets of success? Where could a young man find the road to wealth? Did he have to be a genius? Not at all. In fact, many of the authors noted that being a genius was frequently an obstacle to success since, as everyone knew, the genius was a lazy, vain, impatient, and undisciplined creature. In deprecating genius the authors of the success manuals made abundantly clear that almost everybody could be a success—since almost everybody was not a genius.

But, a youth might ask, what about the environment, did not that play an important role in success? The success handbook did not shrink from this topic and most frankly admitted that certain environments contained more advantages than others. The most widely acclaimed was poverty. The best condition for success was to be born poor. The struggle against poverty, they argued, developed those personal qualities necessary for success. Climbing out of poverty gave testimony to one's worth of character. The greater the climb, the greater the testimony. So the children of the rich, deprived of the very conditions that developed those character traits necessary for success, had less opportunity for success than did the children of the poor. One of the staunchest defenders of poverty, Andrew Carnegie, pleaded: "Abolish luxury if you please, but leave us the soil upon which alone the virtues and all that is precious in human character grow; poverty—honest poverty."

In the race for success those born in rural areas also had a decided advantage, according to the handbooks. A childhood spent in rural life ensured a healthy body and a strong moral character. The fresh air, the good food, hardened one for the rigors of later life while the daily round of chores allowed little time for developing mischievous habits. One clergyman in 1883 reminded readers that: "Our successful men did not feed themselves on boyhood cigarettes and late suppers, with loafing as their only labor and midnight parties for their regular evening dissipation. Such city trained bodies often give out when the strain comes in business, while the sound body and mind and morals of the man from the country hold on and hold out."

In stressing both poverty and rural beginnings, the literature of success reflected, for the most part, the early beginnings of most of the successful men of the times. But, at the same time, these writings were also indicating that success was possible for the majority of people since the majority were poor and had been raised in rural areas. So to play up the advantages of poverty and country life was to play up the great opportunities that existed for most Americans.

Suppose, as was the case for most Americans in the 1880's, one had the dual advantages of poverty and rural beginnings. What then? Certainly a youth needed further guidance. The handbooks supplied this guidance, and the guidance differed little from that given by Benjamin Franklin over one hundred years earlier. (Significantly, a new, ten-volume edition of Franklin's writings appeared in 1887–1888.)

Neither management skills, nor production techniques,

nor investment procedures were the qualities necessary for success; they were to be found within. Moral virtue —this was the key to success. America had not changed. The secrets of success still consisted of the familiar formulas of Franklin: industry, thrift, perseverance. Franklin, of course, had not invented these virtues. Indeed, through the history of western civilization, men have praised these same virtues, especially Christians, and especially Protestant Christians. Through the practice of these virtues one accumulated material wealth and simultaneously identified oneself as one of God's elect.

In American success literature of the 1880's we find a forceful reaffirmation of this synthesis of business success and supernatural grace. William Makepeace Thayer, in 1881, noted that religion required every young man to "make the most of himself possible; that he should watch and improve his opportunities; that he should be industrious, up-right, faithful and prompt; that he should task his talents, whether one or ten, to the utmost; that he should waste neither time nor money; that *duty* and not pleasure or ease should be his watchword." Reliable shops and stores, of course, demanded the same things of young employees. Religion adds "those higher motives that immortality creates." Thayer clinches the union of Christianity and the cult of success with the comment: "Indeed, we might say that religion demands success."

Of all the qualities prescribed for success, none received more attention than the virtue of industry. Wilbur Crofts, in *Successful Men*, revealed that in response to a questionnaire sent to some five hundred prominent men, three out of four attributed success to their own industriousness, to work habits they had cultivated in youth. Idleness, another author wrote, not only doomed men to obscurity and failure; it was a species of fraud upon the community since the idler could not justify his existence. Who then could fail to understand why society condemned idleness?

Once again the moral came through clearly. Success came to the industrious, and who could not acquire this virtue? All Americans, then, had the opportunity to succeed. There were other virtues that helped. "Perseverance," said John D. Rockefeller, "is the great thing." The young man who sticks is one who succeeds. Ultimate victory, the handbooks pointed out, belonged to the man who could plod on in the face of temporary setbacks.

Frugality won acclaim as an additional prerequisite for personal fortune. The spendthrift, all agreed, usually died a poor man. The thrifty man, who saved and invested wisely, not only secured his own private fortune, but became a public benefactor, by providing money for industrial enterprises.

In addition to the magic virtues of industry, thrift, and perseverance, a young man needed to develop those qualities which most impressed employers. The lad who came to work on time always won rewards. Punctuality counted, as did loyalty, and obedience. The loyal and obedient employee caught the attention of the employer when he placed the employer's interest above his own.

III

Most Americans had heard all this before. As children they had read these same notions in their school textbooks. The nineteenth-century readers saturated children with paeans to the land of opportunity while at the same time supplying sage advice about the secret of success.

The schools used a wide variety of different readers, raising the sales of some up into the millions. The most famous of all—"the unprecedented wonder of the publishing world"—*McGuffey's Readers,* sold 122 million copies between 1836 and 1920. The peak of popularity came during the 1870's and 1880's when sales reached over 60 million copies.

The *McGuffey's Readers* from the first to the sixth grades contained stories and tales that admonished American children to be industrious, persevering, thrifty, and loyal. In these readers the idle boy almost invariably turns out poor and miserable; the industrious boy, happy and prosperous. Not just hard-working lads, but insects, like the industrious bee, were exhibited as models. The students of the second reader learned that

> In days that are sunny
> He's getting his honey;
> In days that are cloudy
> He's making his wax . . .
> From morning's first light
> Till the coming of night
> He's singing and toiling
> The summer day through.

The readers stressed perseverance over and over again. One story tells of a little boy who grows disgusted when he repeatedly fails to get his kite aloft. His aunt, however, insists that he try again and again until he finally succeeds. "Yes, my dear children, I wish to teach you the value of PERSEVERANCE. . . . Whenever you fail in your attempts to do a good thing, let your motto be TRY

AGAIN." From an earlier reader the young scholar had already learned:

> If you find your task is hard
>   try, try again;
> Time will bring you your reward
>   try, try again;
> All that other folks can do,
> Why with patience, should not you?
> Only keep this rule in view:
>   try, try again.

McGuffey taught children the worth of obedience by recounting tales in which disobedience brought on disasters like overturned boats or cut hands. The fourth reader has a model of obedience in Casabianca, the boy who stood on the burning deck rather than disobey his father. He died, of course, but Casabianca "would rather die than disobey."

Central to most of the stories, poems, and tales is the theme of rags to riches. McGuffey pictures America as the land of opportunity, where virtue is always rewarded with material success. The second reader contains a typical story about one "Henry the bootblack," who fought against poverty, saving his widowed mother from starvation. The fourth reader featured fatherless Henry Bond, who began to make his own way at the age of ten, when he shoveled snow to get money to buy his schoolbooks. Henry's efforts developed those qualities necessary for success, and from that time on "Henry was always the first in all his classes. He knew no such word as *fail*, but always succeeded in all he attempted. Having the 'will,' he always found the 'way.' "

After working through *McGuffey's Readers*, the American youth of the 1880's was ready to devour the success novels of Horatio Alger. A number of success novelists feverishly published their works during this period, but of all who played the rags to riches theme, none was better known than this one-time Unitarian minister. In the hands of Horatio Alger it received its classic treatment in novels like *Struggling Upward* and *Mark, the Matchboy.*

Alger's first, and wildly popular, *Ragged Dick* appeared in 1867. During the eighties he reached the peak of his popularity, becoming the most famous writer of children's books in the country. Using a sure-fire and unvarying formula, he wrote 106 books for boys, and using the same formula, publishers put out at least eleven other books under his name.

In story after story Alger tells of the poor boy who through pluck, and a little luck, capitalizes on the opportunities available to him and rises to the top. The typical Alger hero is never a genius. He is manly and self-reliant, embodying those traditional virtues of industry, perseverance, honesty, and thrift.

By the eighties, "the Horatio Alger boy" had become an American symbol, the theory of "work and win" synonymous with the name Horatio Alger. During this decade his books flooded the book stalls; copies stocked the shelves of every YMCA in the country. Often copies of these novels were bestowed on children as Sunday School prizes.

IV

Despite the flood of success literature during the eighties, or perhaps because of it, some Americans began to scoff. Although it purported to supply guidance to those aspiring to success, this literature actually did no more than supply reassurance that America had not changed. America—so went the message—was still the land of opportunity. But, of course, America had changed. The world described by these authors had disappeared. Nevertheless, schoolbooks, novels, biographies, and manuals all continued to preach the old formulas for success. The scoffers pointed out that these success formulas had become irrelevant in modern America.

The Horatio Alger hero, for example, always attained success by leaving the working class to become owner or a partner in a business of his own. But few of Alger's heroes have any connection with transportation, mining, manufacturing, or construction—the industries where the successful nineteenth-century men actually made their fortunes. Alger usually rewarded his hero with a partnership in a respectable mercantile house. As John Cawelti has noted, this is "a throwback to the economic life of an earlier period, when American business was still dominated by merchants." The economic behavior of these earlier merchant types was unlike the devastating strategies of transcontinental railroad builders, iron and steel manufacturers, and other corporate giants of the 1880's.

Horatio Alger was not alone in recounting a version of success common to a bygone era. *McGuffey's Readers*, the manuals and handbooks, the biographies of wealthy men, all presented the same mythical version of success. The fact of the matter is that most who rose to the top during this period were not self-made men who started out as poor farm boys, but instead, men who had decided advantages in the race to the top. The typical successful man, as William Miller has shown, was "born and bred in an atmosphere in which business and a relatively high social standing were intimately associated with his family life."

By the mid-eighties the scoffers had convinced a number of people that the old success story was a myth. As a result the men of wealth began to lose some of their luster. In some quarters people now referred to them as the "robber barons." E. L. Godkin had called Cornelius Vanderbilt "a lineal successor of the medieval baron"— and the term stuck. Godkin was one of the first to write that the old mode of making a great fortune "by slowly working one's way up," by frugality, the practices of industry, and the display of punctuality and integrity no longer applied. By the end of the eighties the old mode had indeed fallen into disrepute. Richard T. Ely wrote in 1889: "If you tell a single concrete working man on the Baltimore & Ohio Railroad that he may yet be the president of the company, it is not demonstrable that you have told him what is not true, although it is within bounds to say that he is far more likely to be killed by a stroke of lightning."

The literature of success had not pulled it off. More and more Americans came to admit that the old formulas were obsolete. True, the success manuals continued to be written. In 1894 Orison Marden published *Pushing to the Front*, which subsequently went through 250 editions. The Horatio Alger stories continued to appear, but at the same time the ranks of the scoffers increased.

Some did more than scoff. They rejected this new America, this new society that deprived them of opportunity. "Land of opportunity you say," a Chicago worker snarled in 1887, "You know damn well my children will be where I am—that is, if I can keep them out of the gutter." In radical protest against this new America, many in the late eighties turned to socialism. Socialism had never been a great force in America, but in the aftermath of the great railroad strike of 1877, the socialist movement had begun a steady growth. In Chicago and St. Louis, socialist candidates had actually gained political office in municipal elections. Anarchism too found followers in America. In 1883 the red and black "internationals" issued the famous Pittsburgh Manifesto, expounding the revolutionary anarchist philosophy: "All attempts in the past to reform this monstrous [capitalism] by peaceable means, such as the ballot, have been futile, and all such efforts in the future must necessarily be so . . . there remains but one recourse—FORCE!"

V

More potent than the threat of socialism or anarchism to capitalism during the 1880's was the growing colossus, the Noble Order of the Knights of Labor. It was founded in Philadelphia in 1869 by Uriah Stephens together with some fellow members of a collapsing garment cutters benefit society. The order developed into a national labor organization during the depression. By 1879 it boasted 20,151 members.

The Knights of Labor symbolized a hankering for a simpler economic era, one antedating the wage system of industrialization. Under Stephens, the primary object of the Knights consisted of "educating the public" in order to create a healthy opinion toward labor. When Stephens stepped down as grand master of the order, he was succeeded by Terence C. Powderly who preached a new brand of utopianism: *cooperation.* Envisioning a new America, Powderly believed that through establishing cooperatives, American workers could cross the chasm to the land of the capitalist.

Powderly, however, could not control the large, sprawling Noble Order. The local assemblies, frequently consisting of the members of one trade, preferred strikes to cooperation. So during the early years of the eighties most of the activity of the Knights was spent directing strikes. The most important strike of this period took place in 1883, when the telegraphers struck against all commercial telegraph companies in the nation. Although it gained widespread public sympathy, this strike, like most others at that time, proved unsuccessful. Despite this lack of successful strikes the members of the Knights continued to increase, rising to over 51,000 by 1883. True, the Knights did have a rapid turnover in membership; many came in before and during a strike, then left when the strike proved futile. Over 25,000 left the order in 1883 alone. But the membership did keep rising, and the public now cast an uneasy glance at the dangerous, grumbling giant.

After the long series of unsuccessful strikes, some members were ready to make an attempt to establish cooperatives. They set up workers' cooperatives for mining, for foundries, for the manufacture of shoes, clothing, soap, and furniture. By 1887 the Knights had established 135 cooperatives. But, as would be expected, they soon failed, partly because of inexperience and inefficiency, but primarily because of the discrimination against them from the capitalists, who charged them exorbitant interest rates on loans, refused to transport their goods by rail, and refused to supply them with raw materials.

Before passing out of the scene, however, the Knights played a central role in what John R. Commons has

called the great upheaval of 1886. The build-up began
in the spring of 1885 when the Knights finally had a
real success with strike action. Members of the order
working on the lines of Jay Gould's railroad system
launched an unpremeditated strike against wage reduc-
tions. Taken by surprise, Gould gave way. Later he
attempted a lockout which brought on a second strike;
again Gould capitulated. The prestige of the Knights
soared; membership mushroomed to 700,000. A reporter
for the *New York Sun* concluded that compared with
the leaders of the Noble Order, the power of the President of the United States and of his cabinet "is a petty
authority." The leaders of the Knights, the reporter
warned, "can array labor against capital, putting labor
on the offensive or the defensive, for quiet and stubborn
self-protection, or for angry, organized assault, as they
will."

Many recalled these ominous words when the next
May the Knights of Labor, against the advice of Powderly, supported a general strike. The general strike for
an eight-hour day had been called by a rival labor
organization, the Federation of Organized Trades. Many
workers belonged to both organizations, and most of the
local assemblies of the order voted to strike. Four days
after the strike began, the Haymarket bomb exploded,
shattering the future of the Noble Order of the Knights
of Labor.

On that May 4, a group of anarchists, speaking before
a group of laborers in Haymarket Square in Chicago,
were suddenly set upon by a cordon of policemen who
advanced to break up the meeting. Suddenly a bomb
was thrown at the police. In the melee that followed
one police officer was killed, a number wounded.

Panic and repulsion swept the country. Where will

it all end, people asked. The Knights of Labor, the anarchists, the socialists, all wanted to do away with capitalism, wanted to replace it with some utopian scheme. The country was full of groups of people formulating new utopian schemes. Between 1885 and 1890 forty different utopian novels appeared. Most of these pictured some sort of collectivized society. The most popular of all, Edward Bellamy's *Looking Backward* (1886), sold over a half a million copies in its first decade of publication. Nationalist clubs, inspired by the ideal collective society depicted in the novel, sprang up all over the country.

Were these reformers correct? Was it true that America was no longer the land of opportunity? People were confused. Before the end of the decade, however, a new credo appeared that helped to dispel some of the confusion. According to the new creed America was the land of equal opportunity for all. Once people stopped lamenting the diminished opportunities America now offered and adopted the new creed of equal opportunity, the function of American education had to undergo a profound change.

VI

As early as 1885, the year before the general strike, the Scots-bred Andrew Carnegie publicly admitted that America was no longer the land of opportunity it had been. Speaking to the students of the Curry Commercial College in Pittsburgh, he said: "There is no doubt that it is becoming harder and harder as business gravitates more and more to immense concerns for a young man without capital to get a start for himself, and in this city especially, when larger and larger capital is essential, it is unusually difficult."

The following year, the year of the general strike, Carnegie published his panegyric to American capitalism, which he called *Triumphant Democracy*. Once again he admitted that opportunities in America had diminished. "As the country fills," he explained, "these prizes naturally become more and more difficult to secure." Somewhat lamely he added that these diminished opportunities spur greater effort, "provide additional incentives to make hay while the sun shines."

Triumphant Democracy was essentially a long recital of the material achievements of America. Carnegie bragged how America surpassed the countries of the Old World in agriculture, in manufacturing, in commerce. With regard to education, religion, and art, Americans had more schools, more churchgoers, and more paintings than the countries of Europe. This remarkable material progress Carnegie attributed to the condition of political equality found in America. The removal of the taint of political inferiority—still existent in Europe—had freed the individual. Because of this freedom, some men had become millionaires: "The equality of the citizen is the fundamental law upon which is founded all that brings sweetness and light to human life." An emancipated people had wrought the "miracle of America." As he presented it, America was "Triumphant Democracy."

After tracing the material greatness of America to its condition of equality, Carnegie pointed out that one of the bulwarks of American equality was American education. "The free common school system of the land is," he wrote, "probably after all, the greatest single power in the unifying powers which produce the American race." In these common schools, where all receive the same, good education, "the children of Irishmen, Germans, Italians, Spaniards, and Swedes, side by side with the native Americans . . . are transmuted into republican Americans and are made one in love for a country which provides equal rights and privileges for all her children."

In describing the equalizing function of the common school, Carnegie was merely giving voice to the conception most Americans shared. Horace Mann, "the father of the common school," had declared in 1844 that in America education was "the great equalizer of the conditions of men . . . the balance wheel of the social machinery." Carnegie shared the unbounded faith of his adopted land in the power of education. "Just see," he intoned, "wherever we peer into the first tiny springs of the national life, how this true panacea for all the ills of the body politic bubbles forth—education, education, education."

In his paean to the material triumph of American democracy, Carnegie ignored the complaints from many that this great American wealth was largely in the hands of a very few Americans. Some of these complainers, the socialists, wanted the wealth distributed more evenly, more equally. Carnegie had paid no heed to the socialists in his book. But the general strike in 1886 and its aftermath revealed socialism to be a viable force in American society.

By 1889 Andrew Carnegie had an antidote for socialism. The antidote was a new creed, soon to be called the "gospel of wealth." Carnegie first expounded it in 1884 in the *North American Review*. The article, simply entitled "Wealth," was acclaimed by the editor as "the finest article I have ever published in the *Review*."

Carnegie began his article by dismissing socialism as something from out of the past, something that "belongs to another and long succeeding sociological stratum." The race has tried that, he admonished. We have displaced collectivism with individualism, so to return to socialism would necessitate "the changing of human nature itself—a work of eons." Better then, Carnegie concluded, to hold on to individualism, private property, the law of accumulation of wealth, and the law of competition; these are "the highest result of human experience, the sod in which society so far has produced the best fruit."

After disposing of socialism as an answer, Carnegie turned to the problem that troubled the socialists: the proper administration of wealth. Under capitalism, since great wealth accumulates in the hands of a few, the main problem is the disposal of surplus wealth. Carnegie admits to three possible modes of disposal. He dismisses two of them. He rejects passing it on to the family and bequeathing it for public purposes. He accepts only the third way: to have it administered by its possessors during their lives. This mode, he submits, is "the true antidote for the temporary unequal distribution of wealth." He pointedly remarks that this mode is founded upon "the present most intense Individualism." To carry it out requires "only the further evolution of existing conditions, not the total overthrow of our civilization," as advocated by the socialists and communists. With this mode of distribution of surplus wealth, Carnegie promises an ideal state, one where "the surplus wealth of the few will become, in the best sense, the property of many, because administered for all."

How can rich men administer their surplus wealth for the benefit of all? Carnegie supplies a list of projects.

They can build and support hospitals, parks, meeting halls, even churches. These benefactions would indeed promote the common good, but they also smack of paternalism. Carnegie, however, did not envision the rich men of America as paternalistic philanthropists, especially not philanthropists who would mollify the masses, keeping them satisfied but poor. Carnegie's main hope was to cast the rich men of America into the role of saviors of American opportunity. Men of wealth, he argued, have an obligation to increase and insure equal opportunity for all. For this reason he held that the best way to dispose of surplus wealth was to give it to educational institutions—to give it to universities or, his favorite, to free libraries.

During his lifetime Carnegie set up 2,811 free libraries and gave $20 million to various American colleges and $22 million to the Carnegie Institute of Technology. His largest gift, $125 million, went to the Carnegie Foundation. Carnegie's heroes of philanthropy were men like Johns Hopkins (1795–1873), Ezra Cornell (1807–1874), Charles Pratt (1830–1891) and Leland Stanford (1824–1893)—all men of wealth who founded institutions of higher learning in the last half of the nineteenth century. A special tribute went to Peter Cooper (1791–1883), who had early seen the need and before the Civil War established a technical school in New York City, called Cooper Union. Carnegie cautioned all who advocated radical change—the Communists, the socialists, the anarchists—to ponder the benefits to America that flowed from Cooper Union.

With his "Gospel of Wealth," Carnegie finally confronted the problem that had bedeviled Americans since the Civil War—the disappearance of opportunity. Before this, Carnegie had mouthed the same platitudes about opportunity voiced by the other millionaires. To the students of Curry Commercial College in Pittsburgh in 1884, for example, he had said: "Still, let me tell you for your encouragement that there is no country in the world, where able and energetic young men can so readily rise as this, nor any city where there is more room at the top." But the rising influence of the socialists had forced him to face the fact that opportunity had disappeared and to realize the possible consequences for his adopted land. The socialists called for an equal distribution of the wealth. But the canny Scot realized that most Americans did not really aspire to the equality the socialists promised. Rather than seeking to be equal, most Americans aspired to rise higher than their neighbors, to achieve more success, more power, more wealth.

Since this is what Americans wanted, Carnegie merely pointed out that they could find it only in capitalism, not in socialism. And although capitalism does concentrate wealth in the hands of a few, the best interests of all are promoted, since these few can re-create opportunities for all by distributing the surplus wealth in benefactions that help people to help themselves. Through benefactions to educational institutions, especially to colleges, rich men provide, in Carnegie's happy phrase, "ladders upon which the aspiring can rise." Colleges already did exist in great numbers in America. But if people now regarded them as ladders to success, more would be needed. If he helped to fill this need, the rich man would thereby prove himself to be a defender of equality of opportunity.

The year after he published "Wealth," Carnegie wrote an article entitled, "How to Win a Fortune." Here he pointed out that most of the men at the top of the mercantile, commercial, financial, and industrial worlds had all started out at the bottom. Beginning by sweeping floors and filling inkwells, they had learned "on the job," and then moved up and out on their own. Carnegie supplied a long list of millionaires who had "started out as poor boys and were trained in that sternest of all schools—poverty." Then he made a significant admission to the young men starting out: "It is no doubt infinitely more difficult to start a new business of any kind today than it was."

Carnegie was right. Most everyone thought it was infinitely more difficult now to start a new business. The opportunities in America existed in the already established companies and corporations, and these corporations and companies, as Carnegie noted, looked to the colleges to supply them with the personnel they needed.

In 1903 a group of foreign observers took note of this new development in America. That year the Mosely Education Commission came from Great Britain to study the relationship between prosperity and education in the United States. The investigators reported that everywhere businessmen told them that as late as 1890 few employers hired college graduates, but that by 1900 many had developed a decided preference for the college man. The Pennsylvania Railroad, for example, had recently adopted regulations requiring all future executives to have some college training in engineering. In 1900 the famed corporation lawyer James B. Dill wrote that the "corporate tendency" in American business made college training necessary for success, "because the demand today for trained minds devoted to specific lines of work, has created a demand for college trained men."

By 1900 opportunity in America no longer existed "in the raw." The path to success was becoming much more structured. In the preindustrial days of abundant opportunity, a youth had tested himself and proved his merit "on the job." Now the testing and proving was to take place before he ever entered the world of work. The schools were to take over this task. The youth who climbed the educational ladder would thereby prove his merit and be rewarded with the top echelon jobs.

In order to perform this new function of preparing people for the opportunities now provided in America, the American schools had to undertake a profound transformation, one that took place in the twenty years following publication of Carnegie's "Gospel of Wealth." Once Americans began to look at the schools as central to the economic life of the country, the number and the kinds of schools had to increase. Moreover, these schools had to be welded into a system of education, a ladder upon which the aspiring could rise.

VII

No system of American education existed in 1890. Nor could one find many educators committed to vocationalism. The colleges, especially, remained adamantly opposed to it, and so long as the colleges shunned the career-training function, the idea of an educational ladder to opportunity remained just that—an idea. In 1855 the president of the University of Alabama had written with assurance: "While time lasts, the farmer will be made in the field, the manufacturer in the shop, the merchant in the counting room, the civil engineer in the midst of the actual operation of his science." Since the days of the famous "Yale Report" of 1828 condemning vocationalism in higher education, the colleges had taken this stand, becoming, as a result, more and more irrelevant in American society.

Nevertheless, the colleges continued to hold on to their traditional teaching function: transmitting liberal culture and imparting discipline and piety.

After the Civil War the ideal of research began to make some headway in American higher education, especially with the founding of Johns Hopkins University in 1867. Here, as Frederick Rudolph has written, "the university found its purpose in knowledge, in the world of the intellect." The first president of Johns Hopkins, David Coit Gilman, announced that the functions of the university were: "the acquisition, conservation, refinement and distribution of knowledge." Research, it seemed, had top priority. At the University of Chicago, founded in 1890, the president, William Rainey Harper, was more blunt: "It is proposed in this institution to make the work of investigation primary, the work of giving instruction secondary."

This research movement in higher education brought teaching closer to vocationalism. Ezra Cornell, the founder of the University bearing his name, declared: "I would found an institution where any person can find instruction in any study." With the help of Andrew D. White, its first president, Cornell University opened in 1869 with the expressed aim of uniting "practical and liberal learning." As Laurence Veysey has shown, however, vocationalism did not emerge as the dominant function of higher education until the end of the century. Throughout the nineties, the old and the new conceptions competed with one another. But by 1900 colleges began to welcome future merchants, journalists, manufacturers, chemists, teachers, inventors, artists, musicians, dieticians, pharmacists, scientific farmers, and engineers —training them in the skills of their profession, just as they had always trained the potential lawyers, ministers, and physicians. Departments, and sometimes whole schools, grew up where one could study business administration, forestry, journalism, veterinary medicine, or social work. By the beginning of the century most colleges and universities had been swept up into the movement toward vocationalism. In 1906, E. J. James, then president of the University of Illinois, declared that the state university must "stand simply, plainly, unequivocally and uncompromisingly for training, for vocation . . ." Scholarship was necessary, he added, only insofar "as scholarship is a necessary incident to all proper training of a higher sort of vocation . . ."

By 1900, vocationalism not only dominated all the new graduate programs; it invaded the undergraduate programs as well. Increasingly the undergraduate sought and got a specialist's education. Throughout the land, the traditional prescribed curriculum of the colleges gave way to the elective system, which permitted students to choose courses from a variety offered. Through this freedom of choice the student was supposed to become a trained expert in some special field.

The triumph of vocationalism was hastened by the lavish financial grants to colleges and universities made by the captains of industry. At Columbia University, for example, the philanthropic gifts received between 1890 and 1901 amounted to more than twice the total amount received from its beginnings. The list of donors read like a Who's Who of millionaires: Morgan, Vanderbilt, Havemeyer, Pulitzer, Schiff, Fish. New York University received gifts from Jay Gould. John D. Rockefeller founded the University of Chicago in 1900; he also gave large sums to Brown University. Mark Hanna gave to Kenyon, and George Eastman virtually created the University of Rochester. The money donated by these millionaires enabled the colleges to build the new schools, hire the new professors, and house the new departments. More often than not these gifts were unsolicited by the institutions of higher learning. But gradually there emerged a new breed of college president, one who sometimes solicited these grants or at least sought to administer effectively and efficiently the newly gained wealth of his college. Veblen called these new administrators the "captains of erudition." They were a far cry from the old-time college president, who, usually a clergyman who taught moral philosophy to seniors, now found himself out of date in the new academia. Very few of the new administrators taught classes at all; they were too preoccupied with administering their rapidly expanding empires.

Before the first decade of the century ended, the university had become an American institution, holding out the promise of economic advancement to all who entered. The university now provided the key to opportunity in America. Moreover, there was increased opportunity for all to get this key since by this time the university was widely accessible to all youths. During the same twenty-year period that vocationalism emerged as the primary function of higher education, Americans were creating an educational system. By 1910 the university had become the top rung of the American educational ladder to opportunity.

VIII

Back in 1890, Charles W. Eliot, the president of Harvard University, had complained to the delegates attending the NEA convention that no state in the union possessed "a system of secondary education."

And so long as this gap between the elementary schools and the colleges persisted, no state had what could properly be called a system of education.

To create a system of education, the gap between the elementary school and the college had to be filled by a secondary school that prepared students for entrance into college. This the secondary schools failed to do. President Eliot informed the NEA delegates in 1890 that only nine high schools in all of Massachusetts sent pupils to Harvard College every year. He reported that of 352 students admitted to Harvard in 1889, only 97 had been prepared at free public high schools. Since everyone considered the Massachusetts high schools far superior to those in other states, the conclusion was obvious: free public secondary education was in a sad condition throughout the nation. Plainly the public high schools were not preparing students for admission to Harvard College, or to any other college that had respectable admission requirements.

Eliot, perhaps, expected too much of the high school. Actually the free public high school had only recently come into existence in the United States. Boston had created the first public high school in 1821. But few cities or school districts had followed the lead of the Bostonians. By 1860, according to William T. Harris, onetime U.S. Commissioner of Education, there were but forty high schools in the entire United States. Others dispute this. I. L. Kandel, for example, claims that 321 existed in 1860. Not until 1890 do we have reliable records. In that year the U.S. Commissioner counted 2,556 public high schools. By this time the number of public schools surpassed the total number of private secondary schools (1,632) and enrolled more than twice as many students as the private schools.

The rapid increase in the number of high schools can be explained partly by the fact that the public high schools had become increasingly responsive to different expectations and demands of the people in the local school district. Since most of the financial support for the high school came from the local school district, the high schools had no choice but to become responsive to whatever demands were made. So during this period of rapid growth—from 1860 to 1895—one finds an amazing increase in the number and variety of public high school programs. A study of those in the north central area in 1860 revealed that 12 high schools offered only one course, the classical or Latin course; of the remaining 8 high schools, 6 had only 2 programs, while 2 offered 3 programs. By 1896 the number of high schools in the area had risen from 20 to 60. These 60 high schools offered a grand total of 35 different programs. Only 35 of the 60 high schools offered a single program. Thirty-two of them offered from 2 to 4 different programs, 2 offered 6, and one high school had 7 different programs.

What did these new programs consist of? Back in the 1860's the "general" and "normal" programs had appeared in the high schools, alongside the "classical" program. But now in the nineties one found, in addition to these, such newcomers as the "English and German" program, the "scientific," the "scientific engineering," the "technological" programs, as well as the "commercial English" program.

This tremendous expansion of subjects and programs made the high schools more popular with the masses. But although this expansion had brought about an increase in the number of high schools, at the same time it prevented the creation of an American school system. There could be no school system unless the high schools prepared students for admission to colleges, and the very proliferation of subjects and programs in the high schools had so lowered the quality of education that few self-respecting colleges could admit high school graduates. In his 1890 address to the NEA delegates, Eliot had played up this theme. Because of the inferior quality of the high schools, he claimed, "one half of the most capable children in the United States, at a moderate estimate, have really no open road to colleges and universities." The conclusion was obvious: without a fully completed system of education the schools could never fulfill the function of career preparation.

Most public high school men agreed with critics like Eliot, but they argued that the fault lay with the colleges, not with them. First of all, the college entrance requirements were narrowly conceived in terms of a few traditional subjects: always Latin, Greek, and mathematics, usually English grammar, and sometimes history and geography. But even more disconcerting to the high schools was the fact that subject matter requirements varied so much from one institution to another. Some colleges not only expected applicants to pass a test in Latin, for example, but frequently tested their knowledge of a specific Latin author or even a specific text. Each college had its favorite authors and texts. High school principals across the land complained about the impossible task of preparing students for a number of different colleges, no two of which had the same requirements.

All were agreed on one point: the solution to the problem of articulation of high schools and colleges called for some kind of uniformity. But few Americans, including Eliot, had the temerity to suggest that all the high schools of the land should adopt the same program of instruction. He, however, did formulate one approach to the problem of uniformity in a talk delivered at the NEA convention in 1892 entitled "Undesirable and Desirable Uniformity in Schools." Eliot strongly rejected a prescribed, uniform curriculum, even within a single school, claiming that it "crushes and bruises those priceless individual endowments which systems of education should take infinite pains to bring out." The ideal school, he said, was one that had more different courses of study than any one student could possibly undertake. Eliot was, of course, advocating that high schools adopt the elective system he had so successfully introduced at Harvard.

After dismissing the "undesirable uniformity" of a prescribed course of study, Eliot turned to what he conceived as desirable uniformity. This, briefly stated, consisted of uniform standards of instruction for each course so that all who studied any elected subject would be taught the same topics, for the same amount of time, in the same way, and be given the same tests.

At this 1892 convention the NEA selected a committee, called the Committee of Ten, to investigate the problem of the articulation of the high school and college. As chairman of the committee they chose, naturally, Charles W. Eliot.

The final report of the Committee of Ten did reflect Eliot's ideas insofar as it prescribed no uniform program of studies for all high schools. And while not explicitly endorsing the elective system, it did sanction the basic principle of the elective system, the equivalence of studies. At Harvard College, Eliot had used this principle to shatter the traditional, narrow, prescribed curriculum. At Harvard the elective system had brought about the addition of a wide variety of new courses, all of which counted equally toward a degree. In the report of the Committee of Ten we find the principle of equivalence of studies being used to confine the high schools to a set of nine subject matter areas: Latin, Greek, English, other modern languages, mathematics, physical science, natural history, history, and geography. These nine subject areas were to be considered as equivalent for the purpose of admission to college.

The Committee of Ten proposed a truly ingenious solution to the problem of articulation. Confronted on the one hand with narrow but widely varied college entrance requirements and on the other with a tremendous expansion of high school subjects and programs, the Committee of Ten proposed that the college entrance requirements become wider and more flexible—wide enough and sufficiently flexible to admit students who had followed a program of studies made up of some combination of the nine basic subject matter areas. Then it used this prize of college admission as a lever to get the high schools to restrict their programs to the nine basic subject matter areas.

The committee's report was no less than a blueprint for a type of secondary school that would fill the gap between the elementary school and the college. Once the gap was filled, Americans would have an American system of education—a solidly constructed ladder upon which the aspiring could rise. The committee report put it this way: "A College might say,—we will accept for admission any group of studies taken from the secondary school program, provided that the sum of the studies in each of the four years amounts to sixteen or eighteen, or twenty periods a week,—as may be thought best . . . On the theory that all the subjects are to be considered equivalent in educational rank for the purpose of admission to college, it would make no difference which subject [a student] had chosen from the programme . . ."

IX

The Committee of Ten had no legal power over the schools of America. Yet it did influence the programs and courses in American public high schools. In 1904 Commissioner Harris, who had been a member of the committee, declared that "the scheme of studies recommended by the Committee of Ten on Secondary School studies to the National Education Association in 1893 has become the model for all secondary, or high schools, public and private."

In 1909 the recommendations of the Committee of Ten got support from an unexpected quarter: Andrew Carnegie, or, more precisely, from the Carnegie Foundation for the Advancement of Teaching. The Carnegie Foundation had money to pay pensions to retired professors. This kind of philanthropy would "advance teaching" by encouraging the older and more recalcitrant professors to leave the colleges and create openings for new, young professors more attuned to the changes taking place in higher education.

The Board of Trustees had to decide how to disburse these funds. At that time the Board consisted of three bankers and twenty-two college presidents, including the president of Harvard University, Charles W. Eliot. The trustees decided to pay the pension money directly to the colleges, who would then disburse it to the retiring professors.

By deciding to give the money directly to the college, the Carnegie Foundation put itself into the position of exerting great pressures on the colleges throughout the land. The Foundation proceeded to draw up the standards that a college must meet in order to qualify for the pension funds. It decreed that a college must have at least six full-time professors, a four-year liberal arts course, and a high school course as a requirement for admission. What counted as a high school course? The Board decided that it should consist of sixteen units of 120 classroom clock hours in one subject each. As to the subjects making up these sixteen units, the Trustees indicated their general agreement with the subjects identified by the College Entrance Examination Board (CEEB). The Board, which had been initiated by Nicholas Murray Butler, president of Columbia University, at the suggestion of Charles W. Eliot, had settled upon a list of high school subjects acceptable for admission to college and had established standard tests or examinations in these subjects. The CEEB's list of acceptable subjects differed little from that set out earlier by Eliot's Committee of Ten.

Since most colleges eagerly sought Carnegie pensions, they inevitably pressured the high schools to adopt the "Carnegie unit" as the basis for curriculum construction. Many high schools complied so that within a short time after 1909 practically all high schools measured their work in terms of the unit defined by the Carnegie Foundation.

Yet, in spite of the president of Harvard, in spite of the U.S. Commissioner of Education, and in spite of the Carnegie Foundation—in spite of all that prestige and power—by 1920 only a minority of high school students followed the program of studies proposed by the Committee of Ten. The committee had hoped to provide a blueprint for the entire high school. Why had it failed?

Actually the Committee of Ten had not failed insofar as it did make a college education more widely accessible to all. By inaugurating a course of study in public high schools that colleges would accept, the committee had created greater opportunity for all to enter the ranks of the old and the new professions. But not all available jobs were at this professional level; in fact, most jobs did not require college training. So if the school system was to become a real ladder to job opportunities, then it must train people for these lower level jobs as well as the higher level ones. Obviously, then, the program of studies set forth by the Committee of Ten could not serve as a complete blueprint for the American high school. The committee's program of studies prepared youths for college, but those who did not go to college were disadvantaged by this program since they had to compete in the employment market with other job hunters who had vocational skills. In order to insure equal opportunity for all, the argument went, the school systems had to introduce new and different programs of vocational training.

X

Strident voices had called for new programs of vocational education in the high school back in the nineties. In 1892, Edmund J. James, then a professor at the Wharton School of Finance and Economy of the University of Pennsylvania, delivered a major address before the convention of the American Bankers Association at San Francisco. He called it "A Plea for the Establishment of Commercial High Schools." Four years later the National Education Association welcomed a new group to its fold: the department of business education. At the second meeting of this department, Charles H. Thurber, a professor from the University of Chicago, reported that a survey he had made showed that an overwhelming majority of Chicago businessmen supported the creation of commercial high schools. Within the next few years commercial high schools appeared in Philadelphia and Cleveland, as well as Chicago. By 1899 New York City had established commercial courses in three high schools and that year decided to set up a separate commercial high school.

Reviewing the progress of commercial education in 1899, W. C. Stevenson, of the department of bookkeeping and penmanship of the State Normal School of Emporia, Kansas, boasted to the NEA delegates of the recent "spontaneous sentiment in favor of the commercial high school from all parts of the country for the ninety and nine who go into business pursuits, as well as to the one who goes into the professions of law, medicine, teaching, or to the ministry." The professor from Emporia concluded with a final burst of rhetoric:

> The commercial high school is here. It is based on principles eternal, and is a product of the heart universal. Business is being recognized as more than secularity. Its mission is no less divine than teaching or preaching . . . So long as ambition lives in the hearts of men, or a government exists by the people and for the people, so long will the light of education for use, falling upon the fields of human toil and the pathway of human sorrow, help to transform earth into a suburb of the New Jerusalem.

The delegate from Kansas had given a rousing victory speech; by the end of the century most of the major cities had set up commercial courses and commercial high schools. Here they trained the future clerks, book-keepers, stenographers, and typists. But not all youths were destined for office jobs. What about the blue collar workers? Could the schools train them? Here the school system moved more slowly.

Back in 1879 Calvin Woodward had established the first manual training school in the country. This school, located in St. Louis, had spawned a host of imitators so that by the nineties public manual training schools could be found in Philadelphia, St. Paul, Chicago, Denver, Boston, and Brooklyn.

Calvin Woodward had established the first school to "fit [young men] for the actual duties of life in a more direct and practical manner than is done in the ordinary American School." But in the eighties so many educators attacked the manual training movement for its crass voca-tionalism that its proponents shifted their grounds. Now they pointed up the disciplinary powers of their subject. Through manual training, they argued, the school could educate the whole child, disciplining not only his mind, but his hands as well.

Throughout the nineties, the manual training move-ment continued to grow. In 1894 Massachusetts, for ex-ample, passed a law that required cities of 20,000 in-habitants to include manual training in the high school courses. The manual training educators, meanwhile, took great pains to distinguish their work from technical, trade, or industrial education. Manual training, as they saw it, was a part of general education, not to be counted as vocational preparation. But while these experts in manual training spent time justifying their work to their fellow educators, laymen became increasingly impatient with the impracticality of this kind of schooling.

At the 1899 meeting of the NEA, Charles F. Warren

of the Mechanic Arts High School of Springfield, Massachusetts, pointed out to the members of the manual and
industrial department that "manufacturers are looking
forward to the time when manual training schools can
turn out graduates who are really proficient in some line
of work, and able and willing to join forces with their
employers as producers." Then, after expressing the hope
that he would not be stigmatized as "a deserter from the
ranks of true educational manual training," Warren
offered the timid suggestion that manual training in the
schools be somehow connected with trade education.

Whether in response to Warren, or not, the members
at that 1899 meeting decided to change the name of the
department from manual and industrial department to
department of manual training. But Warren's plea apparently did have some influence since the following year the
department of manual training set up a committee to
study the relations of manual training to trade education.

The work of the committee led to a symposium on
trade education held at the 1903 convention of the NEA.
Here Arthur Henry Chamberlain delivered the most
significant speech. He started off by telling the manual
training educators that they flattered themselves if they
thought manual training had been introduced into the
American schools as a result of the "powerful" educational arguments. "Manual training schools have come
to stay," he declared, "because there is a demand for
that form of education which shall connect itself with
productive industries and with the employments which
the youths of our land are by force of circumstances
bound to follow. . . . It is our duty to appreciate their
full mission and see that they fulfill it."

At this symposium of 1903 few self-respecting educators accepted any longer the theory of mental, or

manual, discipline. Schoolmen now justified school subjects by their practical not their disciplinary value. Speaker after speaker at the symposium pleaded for practical, vocational education. And when the stalwart, old-line defenders of manual training had their chance to respond, many acceded to the pleas for vocationalism. They asked only that the public schools not become "trade schools." They could accept vocationalism so long as the youths were taught, in the words of Woodward, "the processes that underlie a group of trades," not just the processes of a single trade. They argued against trade schools on the grounds that this narrow education, or training, would not prepare youths for a variety of different job opportunities.

But manual training had had its day. In 1906 the Massachusetts Commission on Industrial and Technical Education, called the Douglas Commission, announced that it found widespread indifference to manual training as a school subject. The commission found that many cities disregarded the 1894 law that required them to include manual training in the high schools. It traced this indifference to the narrow views of manual training prevailing among its chief advocates, the educators, who looked upon it as a cultural subject—"a sort of mustard relish, an appetizer—to be conducted without reference to any industrial end." The final verdict was that manual training "has been severed from real life as completely as have other school activities."

The Douglas Commission recommended that all towns and cities provide elective industrial courses in high schools. In addition to day courses for full-time students, they asked cities and towns to provide evening courses for persons already employed in trades, as well as part-time day classes for employed youths between the ages of fourteen and eighteen.

In the fall of 1906, the year that the Douglas Commission gave its report, the National Society for the Promotion of Industrial Education (NSPIE) held its first meeting. The delegates to this meeting selected Henry S. Pritchett as their president. He had been president of Massachusetts Institute of Technology and was currently president of the Carnegie Foundation for the Advancement of Teaching.

According to Pritchett, the underlying purpose of the national society was "the thought that we are no longer fitting our youths for their opportunities in the way in which they must be fitted." Industrial education was needed to prepare young men for the opportunities that America offered. To promote industrial education, the NSPIE brought together industrial workers, manufacturers, schoolteachers, and interested members of the public at large.

The vocational education movement now took on the proportions of a Klondike gold rush. Demands that school systems establish programs of vocational education came from both schoolmen and other public leaders. The movement took hold in great part because the promises held out by its proponents appealed to liberals and conservatives alike. The liberal saw vocational education providing increased job opportunities so that men could become autonomous, no longer victimized by industrialization. The conservative also saw vocational education as the means of providing increased job opportunities, which he found desirable since this would restore stability to American society. He saw unemployed and unoccupied youths as the most serious threat to that stability. If these youths could be kept busy in school, learning something practical that would guarantee employment once they got out, then by all means vocational education was needed.

The NSPIE achieved remarkable success. By 1910 it enlisted the support of *both* the National Association of Manufacturers (NAM) and the American Federation of Labor (AFL) for public vocational schools. Although the high point of the vocational education movement had been passed some five or six years earlier, in 1917 the lumbering machinery of the United States Congress finally passed the first Vocational Education Act. Called the Smith-Hughes Act, it provided federal funds to establish high school vocational programs in agriculture, home economics, and trade and industrial subjects. Although commercial education received no help, the members of Congress had been persuaded to provide support for the vocational training of both boys and girls, for both urban and rural vocations.

So in the twenty years following the publication of Andrew Carnegie's "Gospel of Wealth," the Americans had created a national system of education. What kind of system was it? Did it solve the problem posed in 1884? Did it ensure that all would have equal opportunity for success in America? Did it provide a ladder upon which an aspirant could climb?

XI

When he stepped back to look at the system he had created, the American saw that he had done more than expand and articulate the different schools. He had wrought a change in the function of the American school. Until the nineties, as Carnegie had correctly observed, the American school had functioned as a unifying force, equalizing the children of all citizens. Now the American school functioned less as the "great equalizer" and more as the "great selector." The new, articulated system of education permitted only the most talented to climb to the top of the educational ladder, the ladder that led to the professional jobs. Moreover, the new, differentiated school system not only selected the most talented for the higher level jobs; it selected from the rest those destined for office jobs and those destined for factory jobs. The educational ladder to opportunity really was several ladders. Upon the schools now fell the somewhat awesome responsibility of selecting which one a child should climb.

Charles W. Eliot had made this quite clear in a talk he gave at the 1908 meeting of the NSPIE in which he pointed out that once industrial schools are established, someone will have to decide who will attend them. "Here we come upon a new function for the teachers in our elementary schools," he said, "and in my judgment they have no function more important. The teachers of the elementary schools ought to sort the pupils and sort them by their evident or probable destinies."

This sorting out of people according to their probable destinies was a totally new function for the American school. In the past the American school had not decided the probable destiny of the children who attended it. In America, most people had insisted, a man can take up any job, any occupation: America was the land of opportunity. The idea that any man could take up any job did not mean that any man could do a job as well as any other. Americans did not believe that all men were, in fact, equal. What they did insist upon was that each man should have the opportunity to try his hand at any job he sought. Here they contrasted their land with the countries of Europe, where laws, institutions, and customs denied these opportunities to most men. The Americans had tried to eliminate all such discriminatory laws, customs, and institutions. Moreover, they had relied on the schools to provide all children with a common, unifying experience. Once freed from the artificial restrictions imposed in other countries, once equipped with a common school education, the young American was prepared for the unexpected. He could take up almost any job. But in an industrialized society this just could not be done. Eliot had emphasized this very point in his 1908 talk to the NSPIE. "We must get rid of the notion," he declared, "that some of us were brought up on, that a Yankee can turn his hand to anything. He cannot in this modern world; he positively cannot."

Eliot had made clear what was happening. All now realized that America was no longer the land of opportunity, in the sense that any man could try his hand at any job. But not everyone realized that this meant that the traditional function of the school must also disappear. Not everyone realized that the schools must give up trying to equalize people and concentrate on sorting them out for their "probable destinies." In spite of the convictions of the president of Harvard University, many Americans, especially American educators, felt uneasy about this change in the function of the American school. For the next fifty years most educators refused to accept "career selection" as the primary function of the schools. By various stratagems they were able to deny that the schools selected students for their "probable destinies."

XII

By 1918 some cities had taken a few hesitant steps toward institutionalizing the selection process. Beginning in 1910, first in Berkeley, a number of cities created special intermediate schools called junior high schools where the selection took place. The junior high school, consisting of grades seven through nine, sorted students into one of three courses of study: the general, the commercial, or the industrial. This institutionalized differentiation received official endorsement at the NEA convention in 1915 when the department of superintendence passed a resolution approving "the increasing tendency to establish, beginning with the seventh grade, differentiated courses of study aimed more effectively to prepare the child for his probable future activities."

In addition to attempts to institutionalize the selection process in the junior high school, a number of cities now created a "professional selector"—a guidance counselor. By 1910 there were enough guidance counselors to hold a national conference in Boston. Three years later a National Guidance Association came into existence.

In spite of these attempts to institutionalize and professionalize the career selection function, by 1918 a reaction had set in. That year the NEA's Commission on the Reorganization of Secondary Education (CRSE) issued its final report. Called "The Cardinal Principles of Education," it muted the vocational function of the schools, burying it exactly in the middle of the seven aims of education: (1) Health, (2) Command of fundamental processes, (3) Worthy home membership, (4)

Vocation, (5) Citizenship, (6) Worthy use of leisure time, and (7) Ethical character.

The report of the CRSE did more than mute the vocational function of the schools. It declared that it was subordinate to the traditional function of equalization and unification. The main objectives of education set forth as the seven cardinal principles, for example, were aims for all students. Thus, if all teachers committed themselves to these seven aims, then all students would receive essentially the same education, even though they took different courses of study and prepared for different careers.

The CRSE report recognized the existence of separate courses of study "based on future vocations," but it urged the schools to incorporate various stratagems to equalize, or "unify" the students in these different courses. The report suggested that all students take certain common studies together, like social studies and English. They also suggested that all students should participate in common activities—athletic games, social activities, and the government of the school. Finally, they recommended that all students attend a comprehensive high school—a school containing a variety of different courses of study—rather than separate specialized secondary schools. In the comprehensive school, the report claimed, pupils became "friendly with pupils pursuing other curriculums and having educational goals widely different from their aim." As a result, "the pupils realize that the interests which they hold in common are, after all, far more important than the differences that would tend to make them antagonistic to others."

American educators tried to have it both ways. They would work in a system that selected students for different careers, but the teachers would focus their efforts on the task of equalizing or unifying the students. The compromise, of course, was largely a verbal one. It marks the beginning of the substitution of educational slogans for concrete educational policies in America. No one could argue against the seven cardinal principles of education, for example, but at the same time no one could take these aims seriously as policy to guide practice. They were a slogan, one that educators invoked to convince themselves and others that the schools could, and did, equalize or unify all students.

Other proclamations of common aims appeared in the next twenty-five years, most of them more vacuous hence even less helpful as policy guides than the original seven cardinal principles. In 1938, for example, the Educational Policies Commission of the NEA recommended the following as goals for American education: self-realization, human relationship, economic efficiency, and civic responsibility.

Until the late fifties American teachers refused to accept career training as the primary function of the schools. In their quest to equalize all students they continued to give allegiance to sets of aims for *all* American youth. Moreover, they retained their faith in the prescriptions issued by the CRSE in 1918: common courses for all in general education, common extracurricular activities, and the comprehensive high school. But neither the commitment to common aims nor the emphasis on common experiences succeeded in equalizing or unifying the students. The structure of the educational system—a selective system—defeated all rhetoric and all stratagems.

Study after study of the American schools revealed that they failed to equalize; they merely sorted and selected students for different careers, different ways of life. In their study of a typical midwestern town first in the twenties and then again in the thirties, Robert and Helen Lynd reported that the school system of Middletown sorted out students for different careers. In the twenties they quoted the president of the board of education as saying: "For a long time all boys were trained to be President. Then for a while we trained them all to be professional men. Now we are training boys to get jobs." In the twenties they reported that the cleavage among groups had "become more rigid in the last generation." Nor did the schools of Middletown succeed in equalizing the people during the thirties. When the Lynds returned during that decade, they noted that more children were in school and that they were staying there longer. But rather than equalizing them, the schools were still sorting them out and preparing them for jobs. The Lynds noted that the high school had expanded its course offerings and had inaugurated a complete program of vocational guidance. They credited these changes not to the teachers but to the parents, those "hard-working folk," who wanted "something tangible—a better job, the ability to earn more money—as at least one dependable outcome of 'an education.'"

In the forties, W. L. Warner and his associates studied a number of typical American communities. He reported that even though the schools brought all children together and gave them a common experience and common literacy, one could still see that "as early as ten or twelve, these children all were travelling different paths in life."

In the fifties, Patricia Sexton found that the schools still failed to equalize children. Focusing on "Big City," a large midwestern city, she charted the "inequalities of opportunity in the public schools." She discovered that in the high schools the children from low-income families were almost completely separated from children from high-income families. Children from each group tended to take different subjects and to enroll in different programs. When they took the same courses, the upper-income students were sorted into the higher ability sections of these courses. Moreover, she confirmed other studies, like *Elmstown's Youth*, that reported that the upper-class students dominate the school's extracurricular activities.

Despite the plethora of studies documenting the fact that the schools failed to fulfill the equalizing function, most teachers continued to believe that they could carry it off, if they only tried harder. Even some of the investigators who reported the failures of the schools to equalize students continued to urge teachers to try harder. Some, like Warner and his associates, repeated the familiar prescription of "common educational experiences."

At the same time as the schools failed to equalize their students, some people complained, they failed to do a good job of career preparation. The schools got complaints from factories, from offices, from colleges. The schools, so said the complaints, either improperly selected students or poorly trained them, or both. Nevertheless, the schools, in most instances, did an adequate job of sorting and preparing youths for the factory, for the office, or for a professional career. The selection was not perfect, the training not of the highest quality possible, but, on the whole, the schools did a fairly good job of selecting and training youths for their future careers. However, by the fifties many realized that fairly good was not good enough.

XIII

By the fifties the United States had become what Burton R. Clarke called "the expert society." Industrialization had reached the advanced stage where the service industries increasingly overshadowed the others. From 1900 to 1950 the proportion of agricultural workers in the American labor force had declined from 37 percent to 12 percent; during the same period unskilled laborers declined from 12 percent to 7 percent. On the other hand, skilled and semiskilled workers increased from 23 to 35 percent; clerks and sales workers from 7 to 19 percent. In the fifties these trends accelerated. From 1950 to 1958 alone, professional-technical workers increased from 9 to 11 percent of the labor force.

The rapidly changing occupational patterns spawned a new genre of educational research—manpower studies. During the fifties these researchers confirmed the suspicions of many people when they announced that the United States had too few skilled technicians and professional workers and too many unskilled workers. The need for technicians reached crisis proportions in 1957 when the Soviet Union launched its first sputnik. The Americans transformed this technological defeat into an educational problem. America, too, could launch satellites if it had an adequate supply of trained manpower. In less than a year, the normally sluggish Congress had whipped together legislation to provide federal aid to the schools, appropriately called the National Defense Education Act. This Act provided funds to improve the quality of instruction in the vital areas of science, mathematics, and foreign languages. It also provided funds to expand and improve the guidance and counseling services of all schools. And it supplied funds to enlarge the existing programs of vocational education.

Once the United States Congress had made clear that the primary function of the school was career selection and preparation and proceeded to back up its position with substantial federal funds, many educators came into line. One now heard less about the function of equalizing or unifying all children. Educators now busied themselves "tooling up" the system in order to supply the country with the needed manpower. They now spent lots of time setting up quality programs in the vital subject matter areas, inaugurating special programs for the gifted, and initiating comprehensive programs of guidance and counseling. At the same time they began playing down, even eliminating, some of the old, general education courses—now labeled "the frill courses"—that had supposedly operated to equalize or unify the students.

During this period of rapid transformation some wondered aloud about the comprehensive school. Could it seriously perform this function of career selection and training? Admiral Hyman Rickover declared it could not perform this task satisfactorily and therefore should be abolished. But at this point an old combination appeared on the scene to confer its powerful endorsement on the comprehensive high school.

In 1957 the Carnegie Foundation contracted with James Bryant Conant, former president of Harvard University, to conduct a study of the American school system. Conant issued his first report, *The American High School Today*, in 1959. Here he argued that the comprehensive high school, provided it made some necessary changes, could adequately prepare some students for college, give others a vocational education, and at the same time provide a general education for all. Addressing himself to the members of the local school boards throughout the nation, Conant announced that almost all schools could raise the academic quality of instruction. But more pointedly he called for a sharpening of the selection devices used in the comprehensive high school.

As his first recommendation he insisted that all schools had to improve and expand their counseling and guidance services. He not only recommended that students be grouped according to ability in all subjects but went on to call for complete special programs for the academically talented *plus* an additional special program for the *highly gifted* (estimated as the top 3 percent of the population). Perhaps the most blatant recommendation was the fifth one: the supplement to a high school diploma. "In addition to the diploma," Conant wrote, "each student should be given a durable record of the courses studied and the grades obtained. The existence of such records shall be well publicized so that employers ask for it rather than merely relying on a diploma when questioning an applicant for a job about his education." Here was career selection with a vengeance! "The record might be a card that could be carried in a wallet," Conant added.

As noted earlier, the manpower studies of the fifties pointed up a surplus of unskilled workers as well as a shortage of skilled, technical, and professional workers. The uneasiness this "surplus" problem created found expression in the new concern for the "dropout." Children had been dropping out of schools ever since schools had first opened. In fact, over the half century the "dropout rate" had declined. But now the dropout was a problem; he could not get a job. Therefore, the dropout had to be lured back to school. But once he had been lured back, what could the teachers do for or to him? Most students had dropped out because they could not get along in school. They found the work too difficult or too irrelevant. More of the same could only succeed in driving the returned dropout out of school again, permanently.

James Conant used part of his Carnegie Foundation grant to study this problem. He published his findings and recommendations in 1962 in *Slums and Suburbs*. In the suburban schools he found that since most students go on to college, the main problem these schools faced was to select the appropriate college for each student and to convince the parents of the wisdom of the choice. This problem seemed trivial in comparison with the problem the schools faced in the slums. There, the unemployed, out-òf-school youths had become, in Conant's famous phrase, nothing less than "social dynamite." To preserve the society itself these youths had to be lured back to the schools, where together with other "potential dropouts," they should be taught vocational skills—equipped with what Conant was fond of calling "marketable skills." He recommended that the high schools in the slum areas take on all the functions of an employment bureau, keeping in close touch with the employers and the labor unions, as well as keeping job records for all graduates until the age of twenty-one.

By the sixties public pressures (and financial inducements) from Washington and quasi-public pressures from the Carnegie Foundation helped convince many American educators to accept career selection as the primary function of the schools. In some instances, particularly among the younger teachers, one found that they gravitated toward the career selection function in revulsion against the old slogans, the rhetoric, associated with the equalizing function. These younger teachers, in rejecting the slogans that had justified it, discarded the function as well. A new, hard-headed realism now made its way among members of the teaching profession, including many of the older teachers who had spent much of their professional lives trying to equalize their students. After years of failure they succumbed to disenchantment with the equalizing function, especially as their younger colleagues declared that *they* would not try to do the impossible.

Finally, as one aspect of this hard-headed realism, one sensed that some teachers now actively sought out the role of philosopher-king. Consciously, or perhaps unconsciously, they wanted to have the job of sorting and selecting the next generation.

XIV

Americans had created their educational system at the end of the nineteenth century at a time of widespread lamentation for the disappearance of opportunity in America. The robber barons, the entrepreneurs who "got there first," had accumulated vast wealth, power, and prestige so as to leave no room for the little man to get ahead. To restore opportunity the Americans built a school system, a system to provide, in Carnegie's words, "a ladder on which the aspiring could rise." They expected their schools to guarantee all Americans an equal opportunity for success.

In order for the schools to serve this function, the school system had to be the only ladder to success. Entrance to the top jobs through the back doors of family connections or private wealth had to be sealed off. During the twentieth century this is exactly what took place. The duress of modern technology caused what some have called the corporate revolution—the accumulation of productive property into larger and larger aggregates, the corporations. The corporate revolution undermined the old class of property holders by putting the control over the corporation property into the hands of nonowners—the executives and the managers. These organization men constitute what David Bazelon, in a brilliant essay, has labeled "the new class." One gains entry into this new class through education. People, in Bazelon's words, "translate achieved educational status into organizational advantage." Studies in the sixties revealed that the old "pull" of wealth and family no longer opened the gates of the prestige universities. One study in 1963 of the New York Social Register revealed that "while nearly two-thirds of the men listed went to Harvard, Yale, or Princeton, fewer than half of their sons had done so."

Yet at the very moment the Americans congratulated themselves on creating an educational ladder to the (corporate) land of opportunity, they had to face up to the fact that this same educational system reinforced the gross inequalities already existing in American society. Once they accepted the career selection function built into their school system, they could see that these sorting procedures discriminated against those who had low achievement levels, those who hated school, those with low I.Q.'s. These, the schools selected for the lower level jobs, selected them by allowing them to drop out of the system, by dumping them into some pseudo "vocational training" program.

Since most educators and educated laymen during the sixties had conceded that the child's environment largely determined his school-mindedness, his achievement levels, and even his I.Q., this meant that in the very act of accepting "career selection" as the primary function of the schools, Americans had to face the fact that their school system discriminated against what was now called the "culturally deprived" child. So long as they had refused to accept career selection as the primary function of the school, so long as they had believed that the primary function continued to be equalization, Americans could have faith that their schools were doing something positive for the lower classes. Once, however, they accepted career selection as the primary function of the schools, that faith could not be sustained. The schools did not equalize the lower classes nor did the schools help them to rise. For the culturally deprived the school system now became, to use Paul Goodman's phrase "the universal trap"—a compulsory, selective school system that sorted them out from the competition for the opportunities in America. In 1961 the distinguished psychologist, Kenneth B. Clarke, bluntly stated that the schools of America had become "an instrument of social and economic class distinctions in American society."

What were the Americans to do? Could they persist in developing and improving these instruments of selection that discriminated against the culturally deprived children? Could they continue to busy themselves with ability grouping, tests and measurements, vocational guidance and counseling? As a way out of their dilemma many turned to a stratagem called "compensatory education." This consisted of special supplementary aid, counsel, instruction, and attention for the culturally deprived child. Compensatory education was nothing less than an attempt to use the schools to equalize children, not by giving them all the same "general education" but by making up for their "lacks."

If incorporated fully into the educational system, compensatory education would undermine career selection. But the Americans did not want to destroy the career selection function; they wanted to make it less discriminatory against the culturally deprived. Thus, the most widely implemented form of compensatory education was that provided for preschool children. This kind of compensatory education would not interfere with the career selection carried on by the school system proper. Preschool compensatory education proved so popular that the United States government provided funds to support it throughout the nation, labeling it, appropriately, "Operation Head Start." Educators hoped that if culturally deprived children got a "head start," then the selection and sorting process carried out by the regular school would no longer discriminate against them.

No one expected Operation Head Start programs to eliminate cultural deprivation. But at the same time none, save a few utopian thinkers like Paul Goodman, wanted the schools to abandon the function of career selection. The system was doing a good job in providing opportunities for success to the rest of American youths. For all but the culturally deprived, the school system was still a ladder upon which the aspiring could rise. Those who climbed to the highest rungs could get the top jobs. The system itself, of course, determined who could climb to the top. But this, most people felt, was as it should be. And so in the 1960's, the mass media shouted slogans like, "Stay in School and Get a Good Job!" "Education Is for the Birds—the Birds Who Get Ahead!"

FIVE ‖ THE GOVERNMENT AND THE SCHOOLS

I

Before the Civil War some Americans sought political positions as a means of personal gain. After the war, the floodgates were open, and many, many more sought and secured political offices in order to make money. Graft and corruption became so commonplace that by the 1870's the average citizen used politics as a dirty word and called politicians "spoilsmen."

Many have attributed this upsurge of corruption to the abundant temptations provided by the greatly expanded operations of the government. First the war, then the rapid expansion of business after the war created a multitude of new government jobs. To finance the war the federal government had to hire hordes of new tax collectors, and securing arms and supplies for the troops required an additional army of purchasing agents and government inspectors. After the war the government had to employ many new custom house workers to enforce the high tariffs designed to protect American industry. All of these jobs were filled by the recommendation of a political boss—ward leader, senator, or chairman of the political party. The control wielded by these bosses over such a vast and rapidly expanding empire of patronage opened opportunities for graft, payoffs, and bribes. Moreover, those politically appointed to these public offices frequently exercised their powers in ways that further promoted corruption and chicanery.

The state and local governments also offered many new political jobs. Rising birth rates and increased migration swelled the populations of many cities and states, thereby increasing government responsibilities. The rapidly growing cities added thousands of employees to their payrolls to fight fires, keep the peace, build sewers, install lighting systems, pave streets, administer laws and ordinances. Here, too, all jobs were filled on the recommendation of a political boss. So during this period politicians could become rich by selling jobs, contracts, franchises—whatever they had in their power. As Thomas Cochran and William Miller put it, "politics . . . became one of the great businesses of the nation," and those in politics sought profits "like any other enterprise in a competitive society."

Some of the profits went to support the political machines. In some states, for example, the excise on whiskey filled the coffers of the party treasury. Often the profits went directly to the politician himself, for in addition to selling patronage, officeholders were open to private financial inducements that determined whether or not they would regulate business, tax it, or protect it from regulation or taxation. Since the federal politicians dealt in federal lands, they could sell their favors to those entrepreneurs anxious to build railroads, mine coal and other minerals, drill oil, or sell and settle the empty spaces remaining in America. To secure the necessary land grants, protection, and freedom from regulatory legislation, capitalists donated campaign funds to the politicians, supplied them with investment opportunities, paid them fees, and bribed them outright.

The capitalists spent fabulous sums. In an age of raw competition entrepreneurs vied with one another in bribing the opportunistic politicians in order to gain any advantage over their rivals. According to Hofstadter, the Union Pacific Railroad spent $400,000 on bribes between 1866 and 1872. Few officeholders remained untainted; the graft and corruption seeped deeply into both parties. A Republican senator, Grimes of Iowa, declared in 1870 that he believed his party to be "the most corrupt and debauched political party that ever existed." Few politicians listened, however, since most eagerly sought the rewards of office that only the capitalist could supply. And the capitalist paid no heed since he needed the favors only the politicians could confer. In time, the unlimited greed of the politicians was their undoing. They continued to up the prices for their services and in some instances double-crossed their benefactors. In New York state a classic case occurred when one of Boss Tweed's senators accepted bribes from both Vanderbilt and a competitor in return for his vote on a matter affecting control of the Erie Railroad. Tweed's man voted for the highest donor. By the 1870's many Americans began to call for political reform. The businessman, rebelling against the excesses of bossdom, were especially anxious for some kind of reform.

In 1871, the New York Citizen's Committee, led by corporation lawyer Samuel Tilden, began the campaign that ultimately put Boss Tweed in the penitentiary. In other cities leaders similar to Tilden were organizing crusades against their own bosses. Even earlier in Missouri a coalition of Democrats, dissident Republicans, and Independents had elected a reformer to the U.S. Senate—the highly cultivated Carl Schurz.

In the weekly *Nation* the editor, E. L. Godkin, kept up a continual demand for reform. The root of the evil, he argued, lay not in corruption but in the system. The alliance between industrialists and politicians bred corruption in the form of benefits for business: high tariffs, grants of public land, and federal subsidies. In 1870 Godkin had called for a party "having for its object Tariff Reform, Civil Service Reform, and Minority Representation."

Some of the most avid readers of the *Nation* were what Eric Goldman has labeled "the best people." These came from "families a cut above the middle classes, in which, even if great wealth was lacking, money was no daily problem, a good education was assumed, and the next generation did not have to suffer from the nationality, religion, or reputation of a previous one." These patricians of America considered themselves the national elite, the natural leaders born to rule. But in the new, postbellum America they had been usurped. They saw the country being run by a gang of "spoilsmen" in cahoots with the "new rich," people who lacked the "restraints of culture, experience, the pride, or even the inherited caution of class or rank." The patricians looked about and found themselves in agreement with Godkin's description of America as a "gaudy stream of bespangled, belaced, and beruffled barbarians." Viewing the mad scene, "the great barbecue," the patricians decided to save America. Morality must be restored to political life. The unholy alliance between business and politics had to be severed. Political liberals who seemingly believed in the impartial, neutral state, these patricians-turned-reformers now set out to restore limited government and laissez faire.

They decided to begin at the top. The man occupying the White House symbolized all the evils of the age. Under the administration of Ulysses S. Grant corruption and graft had invaded all branches of all levels of government. "Grantism" had to be eradicated from American life. As the 1872 Presidential election approached, the patricians set out to create a new political party, a liberal reform party, a party that would purify government.

II

The Liberal Republican party held its 1872 convention in Cincinnati. The keynote address by Carl Schurz set the proper tone. The new reform party represented the conscience of the nation. "We saw jobbery and corruption, stimulated to unusual audacity by the opportunities of a protracted Civil War. . . . We saw those in authority with tyrannical insolence thrust the hand of power through the vast machinery of the public service into local and private affairs. . . . We observed this, and . . . the question might well have been asked, 'Have the American people become so utterly indifferent . . . that they should permit themselves to be driven like a flock of sheep by those who now assume to lord it over them?' " This convention, Schurz cried, was the answer.

But the reformers, much to their dismay, soon learned that an age of reform called for more than determination and moral righteousness. It required organization. And the patrician reformers were poorly organized. Their convention had served as a magnet for dissidents of all stripes from the Republican party and a strong contingent from the Democratic party as well. The genuine liberal reformers proved so few in number and so ineffective in the political arena that they failed to keep control of their own convention. The patricians had expected to supply a slate of candidates who had a sense of responsibility to the entire nation, educated men who wished nothing from office save the opportunity to serve the public good. We want men of "superior intelligence, coupled with superior virtues," Carl Schurz declared. In Charles Francis Adams, a patrician's patrician, they found the logical choice for the Presidential nomination. Unfortunately, the convention nominated Horace Greeley, a man opposed to reducing the tariff, scornful of civil service reform, and a vegetarian and prohibitionist to boot.

The landslide election of Grant came as an anticlimax. The American people had answered the patrician reformers. The people wanted none of it. Throughout the nation, Henry Adams wrote, the men of talent, the men of virtue, the natural elite folded their tents and stole silently away.

Not all men of talent gave up so easily, however. Those who persisted in saving America realized that a third political party just would not do; in fact, they now scorned all political parties, seeking to be Independents.

Known to the party stalwarts as "mugwumps," the independent reformers did frequently exert enough influence
to determine the outcome of elections. At the national
level, the two major parties were so equally balanced that
from 1874 to 1894 neither could dominate the federal
government for any length of time. The five Presidential
elections held during this period were all closely con-
tested, with the Democrats losing one, in 1880, by a
mere 7,000 votes. Moreover, throughout these twenty
years a largely Democratic House of Representatives confronted a largely Republican Senate. Only twice did a
single party control both the Presidency and Congress.
Under these conditions the reforming mugwumps could
exert considerable influence. Through exercising discrim-
inating judgment between the major parties, they helped
defeat James G. Blaine's nomination in 1880 and his
election in 1884. They also helped defeat Cleveland's first
bid for a second term in 1888 and did the same thing to
Harrison in 1892.

The mugwump strategy did no more than create a
political stalemate, producing no sustained working majority for twenty years. At the same time this strategy
destroyed the possibilities for any political leadership.
Grover Cleveland, in Hofstadter's words, was "the only
reasonable facsimile of a major President between Lin-
coln and Theodore Roosevelt." In addition to obstructing
all bids at strong leadership, the mugwump strategy did
not produce the kind of legislation the reformers sought.
Although some reform legislation was passed, it did not
destroy the unholy alliance between politics and business.

The principal bond between these two spheres was
the high tariff, and when a bill finally emerged from
the mysterious recesses of the Senate as the Wilson-
Gorman Tariff, it did not reduce the tariff; in fact, it

incorporated increases from 10 to 300 percent on some items. The politicians continued to protect American businessmen. A second bond connecting politics and business consisted of the favors, immunities and privileges the politicians extended to the giant corporations, the "trusts," which included the railroads. Between 1874 and 1885, more than thirty measures for the regulation of interstate railroads were introduced in Congress; all died in the Senate. Finally, during the first Cleveland Administration, the Interstate Commerce Act set up a federal commission to regulate the railroads. But, as Cleveland's Attorney General, Richard Olney, assured the president of the Chicago, Burlington, and Quincy, the act satisfied "the popular clamor for government supervision of the railroads at the same time that that supervision is almost entirely nominal." As Olney predicted, the act became "a sort of barrier between the railroads and the people and a sort of protection against hasty and crude legislation hostile to railroad interest." Finally, during the election year of 1890 Congress passed a bill to regulate the trusts, the Sherman Anti-Trust Act. But this act too was a sop to the reformers, being easily circumvented by the capitalists; in fact, they used it as an effective instrument to combat labor organizations.

Although the mugwump strategy failed to produce legislation adequate to the task of destroying the links between politics and business, there was another tactic that did much to purify politics—civil service reform. At all levels of government, civil service jobs were regarded as the spoils of office that the victorious party expected to distribute as patronage to party stalwarts. The liberal reformers wanted to distribute these jobs on the basis of competitive examinations. Expectedly, they met with furious opposition. But when President Garfield was assassinated by a disgruntled office seeker, a shocked Congress in 1883 passed a Federal Civil Service Law, the Pendleton Act, and a number of states and municipalities followed the lead of the federal government.

This merit system struck at the very root of party power. At the same time it provided entry into public service for those men of "superior intelligence, coupled with superior virtue." Finally, civil service examinations circumvented popular deliberation. The reformers now could secure public office without depending upon the voters. After the fiasco of 1872, the liberal reformers had lost all faith in the intelligence, virtue, or even good will of the masses. They realized, too late, that they had placed too much faith in democracy, had relied too much on popular deliberation. Popular deliberation had cost them control of their political convention; it had returned Ulysses Grant to the White House. The liberal reformers now agreed that the people could never be trusted to elect men of superior intelligence and virtue to public office. This fear of popular deliberation, which amounted to a fear of expanded democracy, is clearly revealed in the way the liberal reformers approached education. After the debacle of their Liberal Republican party, the reformers turned to education—to the schools—not with the hope of raising the level of popular deliberation, but with the intention of curtailing it.

III

Probably the most direct expression of the liberal reformers' educational creed came from Carl Schurz in his Phi Beta Kappa oration at Harvard in

1882. A republic like the United States, he explained, needed two levels of formal education: "the elementary popular education which does not impart a high degree of knowledge, itself, but makes . . . men open, accessible, susceptible to the influence of superior knowledge and culture when they come in contact with it; and that higher education which enables and incites . . . those to whom it imparts superior knowledge and culture, to make their influence felt. No one did more to implement this educational creed of the liberal reformers than America's foremost educationist, William T. Harris.

Born in New England, Harris moved to St. Louis in 1857, after attending Phillips Andover Academy and Yale College. In St. Louis he taught school, rapidly rising to become superintendent of schools in 1868. Harris was more than an educational administrator. A member of the famous St. Louis movement in philosophy, founder and editor of the *Journal of Speculative Philosophy*, he was one of the leading philosophers of his age. Like his philosophic-minded friends in St. Louis, Harris considered himself a disciple of Georg Hegel, a philosopher that nineteenth-century Americans regarded as a political liberal, a spokesman for the republican movement in Europe. According to one commentator, one reason for the popularity of Hegel's philosophy in the United States was that many Americans, including the members of the St. Louis movement, saw it as a philosophy that both explained and healed "the tragic dialectic of the civil war." In accordance with the dialectical progress of civilization, the Hegelians had philosophical certainty that the North and South would now reunite.

When Harris applied Hegel's philosophy to American education, he did no less than articulate the American liberals' conception of the political function of the school.

The school, Harris taught, had four cardinal duties to young children: to train them in the habits of regularity, punctuality, silence, and industry. Unless he had these habits, the child could not adjust to the social order. For Harris the school was the "nursery of civilization," "the center of discipline" that helped to preserve and guarantee the continuation of the social order. As superintendent of schools in one of the nation's largest cities, he saw at firsthand that the urban newcomers lacked these necessary social virtues. In his schools he insisted that the children must learn to accept authority. Through direct moral training of the will the pupil got used to "the established order" and obeyed it "as a habit." Moreover, the child would try to maintain that social order after leaving school, "whether he has ever learned the theory of it or not."

Harris, however, insisted that this direct disciplining of the will had limited efficacy, and he advocated it only for very young children. Ultimately he wanted the child brought to the point of freely and voluntarily accepting discipline and authority. For this to happen, the child had to appreciate the underlying rationality of social existence. As a Hegelian, Harris held that whatever was rational was necessary. So, as he said in one of his St. Louis school reports, education emancipated by giving insight into the origins and function of the " 'conventionalities of society'—thus into their necessity."

The school's job was to supply the child with the tools that enabled him to appreciate the common stock of ideas and cultural values of the civilization of which he was a part. Harris called these tool subjects "the windows of the soul." He listed them as: grammar, the mastery of the word; arithmetic, the mastery of numbers; geography, the mastery over place; history, the mastery over time.

Once he had mastered these subjects, the student could approach the world of intelligence, studying the literature and art of his civilization. Once he perceived its underlying rationality and accepted his culture, once it had become "a living reality," the child could participate in that culture—no longer isolated, no longer alienated.

To be prepared for the exigencies of modern life, the child had to gain insight into the reasonableness of moral commands. Harris was quick to point out that this was a political necessity in America. If the schools aimed for unreasoning obedience from their pupils, they were preparing future adults who would give unreasoning obedience to a demagogue or to a leader in crime. So without the proper education, the masses, especially the immigrant masses, would remain alienated, corrupting the body politic. In a speech delivered to the NEA in 1874 Harris explained that "all the evils which we suffer politically may be traced to the existence of an immense mass of ignorant, illiterate, or semi-educated people who assist in governing the country while they possess no insight into the true nature of the issues which they attempt to decide."

Combining the skills of the practical schoolman with an intensely idealistic philosophy, Harris was, in Lawrence Cremin's words, "the commanding figure of his pedagogical era." In 1889 he became U.S. Commissioner of Education, serving in this position until 1906. Few people have ever had such widespread influence over the American schools. At the time of his death in 1909 a contemporary observed that Harris was "the most quoted," "the best loved," "the most widely known," and the most influential "educator in this or any other country." In him the liberal reformers had found a vital force, one that made reasonable Charles Francis Adams boast to a political club in New York City that: "we do not care which [party] is in office and which is in opposition . . . we who manage the schools, the press, the shops, the railroads, and the exchanges . . . are moving this country, you run the political machine."

In the last decades of the nineteenth century the liberals had control of American education from the bottom to the top. Under the forceful guidance of William T. Harris, the American schools now prepared citizens who accepted rational authority, citizens who accepted the leadership of men of superior intelligence and virtue. To complement the influence of Harris on the schools, the liberals had in their camp the most important man in higher education, the president of Harvard University, Charles W. Eliot.

IV

Charles W. Eliot was a patrician to the core. He was born in Boston in 1834 to a family that traced its roots in New England back to the late seventeenth century. For generations the family name had been familiar to Harvard students. Charles' grandfather, a prosperous merchant, had founded the Eliot Professorship in Greek. His father had served as treasurer of the university. One cousin, Charles Eliot Norton, was an established Harvard professor; another cousin served as a member of the Board of Overseers. With these family ties, no one thought it strange that young Charles became an instructor in mathematics at Harvard, after receiving his B.A. from that institution in 1853. Then, after President Hill resigned in 1868, no one was too surprised to hear that the Board of Overseers had selected the thirty-five-year-old Charles Eliot for the job of president.

At the time of his appointment to the presidency, Eliot held a position at Massachusetts Institute of Technology as a professor of chemistry. This M.I.T. background made some of the Harvard faculty uneasy—the arts people feared having a scientist as president, the scientists worried about having as president a man from a school of technology. Reluctantly, they finally approved the appointment. Within three years their new president had reformed the law school, purged the medical school, and established a graduate school.

Before appointing the new president, the Board of Overseers had expressed the desire to transform Harvard into a "noble University," a "seat of learning which shall attract the best teachers and most ardent students, a university which shall retain all the good of the past and go forward to welcome the advancing light of the future." When they elected Charles W. Eliot, they picked the right man. In his inaugural address he presented a declaration of beliefs that guided him for his forty years as president. Not that Eliot had any master plan for Harvard University in 1869. He merely expressed his firm commitment to the task of transforming Harvard into a great, national institution. Doctrinaire, firm, supremely self-assured, the young president proceeded to turn Harvard University over "like a flapjack." At a meeting of the medical faculty where new reforms were proposed, one of the senior professors asked: "How is it that this faculty has gone for 80 years managing its own affairs and doing it well—and now within three or four months it is proposed to change all our modes of carrying on the school?" Eliot, who was present, immediately spoke up: "I can answer [the doctor's] question very easily. There is a new president."

There was a new president, and he was strong and

determined. By 1871, three years after taking office, he had reorganized the medical school. Instead of getting their salaries directly from their students' lecture fees, as had been customary, all medical professors now received regular salaries from the university, and students paid regular tuition fees to the university. Eliot initiated stiff entrance examinations where none had existed before. Prior to his reforms, a future physician had only sixteen weeks of required attendance at lectures. The only examination he took was a final oral, where he had to receive a passing grade from five of the nine professors who quizzed him for ten minutes each. Eliot asked for, and got, a required three-year course of study for all candidates together with a series of written examinations to be taken at the end of each year.

Other universities soon copied the reforms Eliot inaugurated at Harvard. Medical schools were soon set up on this model at the University of Michigan and the University of Pennsylvania. And in similar fashion, other institutions followed the lead of Harvard in reforming their law schools. In 1870, Eliot brought Christopher Langdell into the school that three practicing lawyers had been conducting as the Harvard Law School. With Eliot's encouragement and support, Langdell drew up a three-year course of study, replete with written examinations. Most important, he introduced the revolutionary "case method" of studying law. By 1893 Christopher Langdell had become the first dean of the Harvard Law School, making it the first graduate school of law in the nation.

After revolutionizing both medical and law education, Eliot created in 1872 a third professional school, the Graduate School of Arts and Science. Now the serious student, instead of going abroad for his advanced train-

ing, could study and prepare for a Master of Art degree
or a Doctor of Philosophy degree at Harvard University.
Harvard could not claim a first here, however. Yale University had established, twenty years earlier, a graduate
school of arts and science, which remained definitely
subordinate to the undergraduate program. Would this
be the case at Harvard? Wasn't there a real danger that
a graduate school would weaken the college? Eliot, as
always, had a ready answer. The graduate school, he
said, "will strengthen the college. As long as our teachers
regard their work as simply giving so many courses for
undergraduates, we shall never have first-class teaching
here. If they have to teach undergraduate students as
well as graduates, they will regard their subjects as infinite and keep up that constant investigation which is
necessary for first-class teaching."

Under Eliot's guiding hand, Harvard did become a
great national university. True, reforms in the medical
and law schools resulted in an initial decline in enrollments. This brought a typical nostrum from the unflap-
pable Eliot: "the only way to drive people out of a school
permanently is to let it be a poor school." He was, of
course, correct, and before the end of the seventies enrollments in both schools had risen above the pre-reform
days. Most important, the number of students from outside the New England area had doubled. By the end of
Eliot's forty-year tenure as president, Harvard had become the largest and wealthiest university in the country.
In 1869 he had inherited a faculty of sixty; he be-
queathed one of 600. When Eliot took office, Harvard
had an endowment of $2 million; when he left, that
endowment equaled $20 million.

Of all his reforms none did more to transform Harvard
University than the undergraduate elective system. This,

Eliot said in 1894, "has proved to be the most generally useful piece of work which the university has ever executed." Electives existed at Harvard University before Eliot came on the scene, but as peripheral subjects, inferior to the prescribed studies. Eliot proceeded slowly but surely to abolish all prescribed subjects, finishing the job in the nineties. This extension of the principle of election to the exclusion of all prescribed subjects rendered all subjects equal—the notion of equivalence of studies. Under the "radical electivism" of Eliot, students were free to choose their own course of studies.

While many commentators, including Eliot's immediate successor, President Lowell, have complained about the quality of the education Harvard students received, or elected, under this system, few have noted the impact of this elective system on the quality of education that Harvard professors provided for students. Radical electivism was a lever that Eliot used to widen the scope and increase the depth of studies pursued at Harvard. In this laissez faire atmosphere, each course, each professor, each department was in competition for students. To secure students one had to be a top-flight teacher, and have something meaningful and significant to teach. In addition to improving the caliber of instruction, free, or radical, election brought about an enormous increase in the number of subjects, courses, and faculty. This meant that the Harvard undergraduate could receive a broader and a deeper education than ever before. Nevertheless, to many professors the elective system was a form of blackmail. They opposed a system that had such built-in pressures—on their subjects, their courses, their teaching, their very personalities. Their most effective argument was that American college students were too immature to choose wisely; they chose courses flippantly, or in accord with the laxity or popularity of the professor. These opponents assumed an ideal of the educated man, which, they said, was not being attained by students freely electing their courses of study. Eliot, of course, had his own ideal of the educated man: the expert. Indeed all of his reforms—the professional schools, the graduate school, and the elective system for undergraduates—were of a piece. All contributed to the creation of experts.

In establishing an institution of higher education that functioned to train experts, Charles Eliot differed from most of the liberal reformers of his day. They, for the most part, looked to the college to turn out an elite steeped in the genteel tradition—men of culture, men of virtue. These educated men, they felt, had claim to authority not because of any technical competence but because they possessed a liberal education, which gave them general competence and the right to lead. Eliot, who was more aware than most of the changing times, maintained that the college graduate's claim to leadership must be based upon technical competency. He constantly argued that the American failures of government—at all levels—could be traced to the refusal to employ experts. "The democracy must learn," he argued, "in governmental affairs, whether municipal, state, or national, to employ experts and to abide by their decisions." Like other liberals, Eliot sought to restrict popular deliberation. But he not only distrusted the masses to run the government, he also distrusted the "educated man" who had no expertise. "Such complicated subjects as taxation, finance, and public works, cannot be wisely managed by popular assemblies or their committees," he cautioned, "nor by executive officers who have no special acquaintance with these most difficult subjects."

As Eliot saw it, unless the universities trained experts,

there would be no check on the masses. The liberals had placed their faith in the power of elementary education which would make the masses, in Carl Schurz's words, "open, accessible, susceptible to the influence of superior knowledge and culture when they came in contact with it." But Schurz had not explained just how this was to be done. William Harris, on the other hand, had relied upon a Hegelian faith that the authority of the elite would be a rational authority that the masses, trained to "reasonable obedience," would accept. Lacking Harris' Hegelian faith, Charles Eliot wanted elementary (and secondary) schools to make the masses aware of their limitations. Then, he concluded, they would be willing to trust most of the tasks of government to the experts. The masses could be made aware of their limitations if the schools would concentrate on training them how to think. Once people learned the importance of accurate observation, exact description, and correct inference, then they would "naturally acquire a respect for these powers when exhibited by others in fields unknown to them." The man who has been trained to think will recognize that his own competence is limited to a few subjects and "will come to respect and confide in the experts in every field of human activity."

Perhaps because he never held political office, Eliot clearly saw that one need not hold political office in order to exert political influence. He realized that legislators and administrators increasingly came to depend upon "the researches of scholars, men of science, and historians and follow in the footsteps of inventors, economists, and political philosophers." These experts he felt, were the ones who exerted the real power in America. But Eliot was not so naïve as to discount the importance of institutions as well as men. He realized the political power of a great institution like Harvard University. By fulfilling his commitment to make Harvard University into a great national institution, Charles Eliot provided the surest guarantee that people would listen when one of its experts spoke—be he an alumnus, a professor, or the president.

V

In 1906, William T. Harris retired from his post as U.S. Commissioner of Education. Three years later he died. In the same year Charles W. Eliot stepped down from the presidency of Harvard University. An educational era had ended. The influence on education these "liberal reformers" had shared now passed to a new band of reformers, called progressives. Like their predecessors, these new educational reformers took their cues from the political scene, turning to the schools to help solve political problems.

The political problems in America had altered in the years since 1870 when the liberal reformers had zeroed in on political corruption. They had divined the root of this corruption in the unholy alliance between the businessmen and the politicians. But as early as the 1890's things began to change. By then many of the infamous spoilsmen had passed to their just rewards. At the same time, many businessmen, fed up with paying ever-increasing amounts of money to the politicians, decided to enter politics themselves. In 1888, for example, a New York banker, Levi Morton, entered the White House as Benjamin Harrison's Vice-President. Moreover, the cabinet of this administration included the merchant John Wanamaker, and Redfield Proctor, the so-called marble king of Vermont. People called it the "Businessman's

Cabinet." The entrance of businessmen into politics was even more pronounced in the Senate. This body came to be called the "millionaire's club." There one found lumbermen, bankers, industrialists, publishers, and railroad magnates. These businessmen senators rapidly became a ruling clique that, according to Thomas Cochran and William Miller, "controlled every bill that tried to run the gauntlet of the Senate." The highpoint of this period came in 1896 when Mark Hanna, a capitalist turned political boss, maneuvered William McKinley into the White House.

This emergence of business politics in the eighties and nineties was not precipitated solely by the businessmen's reluctance to continue paying the politicians. The businessmen's decision to enter the political arena was also due to their fears of the increasing agrarian discontent. During the eighties and nineties, the farmers became louder and louder in their denunciation of the existing economic order. They had begun to complain right after the Civil War when farm prices began to decline. Some analysts explained the low prices in terms of the law of supply and demand: the farmers had increased production, so the selling price, naturally, went down. But the farmers would have none of this. They blamed their plight on the middlemen—the railroads, the grain elevators. The cost of storage and transportation ate up all their profits. Frequently the complaint was heard that it cost a bushel of corn to send a bushel of corn to market. There were other villains. The manufacturers of farm equipment—protected from foreign competitors by the high tariff—charged exorbitant prices for their wares, the farmers argued. Another group that took advantage of them was the bankers and moneylenders. They had steered the economy into a strict hard-money policy which worked adversely on debtors.

It was the vociferous complaints of the farmers that had induced Congress to pass the legislation purported to eliminate these evils: the Interstate Commerce Act (1887), and the Wilson-Gorman Tariff Act (1894). As noted earlier, none of these laws did what they were supposed to do. This, naturally, fanned the flame of agrarian discontent, and in the nineties the farmers turned to politics themselves, forming a People's party. This Populist party called for truly revolutionary changes, including public ownership of the railroads, a drastic lowering of the tariff, and an inflationary monetary policy based upon free silver.

The radical thrust of the Populists, which in the South included a Negro-white coalition, frightened many Americans into voting against them. The 1896 election sealed their fate when the American people rejected the Populist candidate, William Jennings Bryan, and chose instead the businessman's president, William McKinley. After this abortive escapade, the Populist party disappeared from the scene. But the evils that the Populists had decried continued to haunt the American public. The accusations the Populists had made could not be ignored: Political power had fallen into the hands of the rich. The United States was ruled by a plutocracy.

In the last years of the nineteenth century, these charges gained more credence as the people witnessed the proliferation of gigantic, monopolistic corporations. In 1898 there were 82 trusts in America. Within the next six years 234 additional trusts appeared, with a capitalization of over $6 million. These trusts included such giants as Consolidated Tobacco, Amalgamated Copper, American Smelting and Refining, and largest of all, United States Steel.

Could this plutocracy be destroyed? For that matter, should it be destroyed, or would its destruction serve to destroy America itself? The Populists had wanted to destroy the plutocracy. They had aimed for a revolution. But the voters had rejected them because of the fear that such a revolution would undermine the very progress and prosperity Americans had enjoyed since the Civil War. Was reform compatible with progress? It was their affirmative answer to this last question that hurled the progressives into political prominence.

VI

Theodore Roosevelt, perhaps the leading progressive politician of the era, sincerely believed in the compatibility—the necessary connection—between progress and reform. He distinguished, for example, between "good trusts" and "bad trusts." In 1902 he said, "Our aim is not to do away with corporations; on the contrary, these big aggregations are an inevitable development of modern industrialism, and the effort to destroy them would be futile unless accomplished in ways that would work the utmost mischief to the entire body politic . . . We draw the line against misconduct, not against wealth." Roosevelt argued that regulation rather than dissolution was the answer. "The government," he wrote "must now interfere to protect labor, to subordinate the big corporation to the public welfare, and to shackle cunning and fraud exactly as centuries before it had interfered to shackle the physical force which does wrong by violence . . ." In pursuing his policy of regulating "bad trusts," he carried out forty-three proceedings for violations of the Sherman Anti-Trust Act.

The progressives stood for increased governmental powers of regulation and control. Roosevelt called for effective regulation of railroads, for federal child-labor legislation, direct income and inheritance taxes, curbs on labor injunctions, federal inspection and regulation of foods and drugs, and protection of the nation's natural resources. He got some of his demands, but some had to await the progressive administrations of his successors, Taft and Wilson. Their administrations expanded and strengthened the power of the government to control the trusts; they also lowered the tariff and reformed the banking credit and currency system.

The federal government was not alone in its attempt to protect the American economy from domination by the plutocracy. The state governments caught up in the progressive movement, passed legislation to protect workers and employees from exploitation. With Wisconsin and Oregon usually leading the way, state legislatures passed laws to curtail or regulate the child and female labor laws, to establish health and safety standards in industry, laws setting up minimum wages and maximum hours, laws providing workmen's compensation.

During this period progressivism also dominated local or municipal government. Here too, the reformers expanded the powers of government to restrict and curtail the plutocracy. Led by reformers like Tom Johnson, mayor of Cleveland from 1901 to 1909, the progressives called for, and frequently got, public ownership of the streetcar system and other utilities that served the cities. They passed new municipal tax laws to replace those that granted privileges or immunities to the plutocracy.

In a special sense, as Richard Hofstadter has shown, the progressives were the spiritual heirs of the liberal reformers. But they differed from them in one crucial respect. The liberals had wanted to restrict governmental power. Only in this way, they thought, could the unholy alliance between politics and business be destroyed. The progressives, on the other hand, wanted to expand government power. They wanted the government to regulate, control, and restrict the powerful business interests. The progressives were the first to denounce the doctrine of limited government and laissez faire. In practice few government administrations had successfully adhered to this doctrine, but none had ever rejected the doctrine itself. From the beginning, Americans of all political persuasions had opposed the idea of strong government. They had traditionally equated strong government with tyranny. But now at the end of the nineteenth century the progressives pointed out that the plutocrats, in fact, had become the tyrants in America. Moreover they insisted that the government was the only institution able to resist or eliminate the powerful plutocracy.

Americans, however, would not give up their commitment to weak government without some guarantee that a strong government would not itself become tyrannical. Here we come to the heart of the progressive movement, the essence of its political philosophy. If the American democracy became truly a democracy, the progressives argued—if the people participated more fully in governmental decisions; if they, in short, became the government itself—then the perennial fears of strong government would disappear. The people could not fear government if they were themselves that government. The genius of progressivism lay in its adoption of a wide variety of strategies to increase public participation in political and governmental decisions. The progressives did not invent all of these devices. Some they copied from abroad, like the Australian secret ballot; some they stole from the Populists, like the direct primary and the initiative and referendum. These devices, used at all levels of government, would permit the people to participate in direct democracy.

Across the nation, progressive reformers in the cities fought for and got municipal home rule. This right to form their own charters permitted many cities to inaugurate direct democratic practices—the initiative, the referendum, and recall of public officials. At the state level, some states not only adopted the direct primary, the initiative, and referendum, but went on to set up commissions, committees, and leagues of interested and knowledgeable citizens as part of the government machinery. Under the progressive governor Robert La Follette, for example, the state of Wisconsin established a railroad commission as well as an industrial commission to regulate health and safety conditions in the future. At the national level, the progressives secured two amendments to the constitution that served the cause of direct democracy; one, the seventeenth amendment, provided for the direct election of senators; the other, the nineteenth, gave nationwide suffrage to women.

The progressives' theory of direct democracy assigned a central role to the schools. Americans had long insisted that a democracy required an educated citizenry. Now the progressives' hope of creating a direct participant democracy meant an even greater demand for an educated citizenry. The very success of this direct democracy depended on the schools. To fulfill this political function, the schools now required a new, progressive theory of education.

VII

So long as they had insisted upon weak government, Americans had to contend with the danger of anarchy, and they had depended upon the schools for protection. The common schools—free and open to all—had the task of taming, civilizing, Americanizing all who attended. In the common schools the schoolmaster molded, shaped, and formed the character of the young, training them so that later as adults they would abhor anarchy. This education would produce citizens who would live in an orderly, law-abiding way in a society that was free from the coercion of a strong government. Foreign observers had noticed this strange American commitment to "anarchy plus a schoolmaster." De Tocqueville, for example, had noted in the 1840's that "in the United States politics are the end and aim of education." He also pointed out that "in the United States instruction of the people powerfully contributes to the support of the democratic republic; and such must always be the case, I believe, when the institution which enlightens the understanding is not separated from the moral education which amends the heart."

When in the twentieth century the progressives abandoned limited government, this link between the schools and democracy became even more crucial. Once the government was free to grow and become strong, the danger of anarchy disappeared. But in its place arose the danger of governmental tyranny. And, as we have seen, the progressives hoped to ward off this danger by creating a participant democracy so that the people themselves became the government. Many progressives realized that if people were ever fully to anticipate and contribute to the processes of government, then a new kind of education was called for. A participant democracy needed schools that would release and unblock people, schools that could uncover and help develop the capabilities and talents of every citizen.

The old education, that traditionally given in the common public schools, tried to tame the child and mold him into a respectable person who controlled his passions. Frequently his school experience repressed the child and stifled his talents. The progressives urged the schools to forget their traditional role as "the great stabilizer" of American society, in favor of a new role as "the great liberator." The progressives believed that once the schools helped the child realize his own particular talents and abilities, once the school "liberated" him, then he could make a more worthy contribution to the political life of the society, enriching the quality of direct democracy.

In this new quest to liberate the child, American educators began to advocate what has been labeled a "child-centered" theory of education. This child-centered theory had first been voiced by Jean Jacques Rousseau in the eighteenth century when he advised teachers to begin "by making a more careful study of your scholars, for it is clear that you know nothing about them." In *Emile*, Rousseau had charted the normal, or natural, development of children, which, he insisted, should guide educational practices. But his conception of human development had been purely speculative, based upon his own limited experience. After the time of Rousseau a science of human development came into being, a science greatly influenced by the theories of Charles Darwin. These scientists of human development saw the child as an evolving organism, and they hoped to determine scientifically just how the child evolved. Once educators knew how children developed, they would be better prepared to foster and aid that development by clearing away obstacles that might block or retard it.

One of the most influential of these scientists of human nature was G. Stanley Hall, a psychologist, once referred to by a contemporary as "the Darwin of the mind." Human development, according to Hall, followed the general psychonomic law which stated "ontogeny recapitulates phylogeny." This meant that as the individual organism, the child, matures, he recapitulates the evolution of the human race, going through the same or similar stages that the race itself had gone through. By means of numerous questionnaires, Hall accumulated a mass of data to support this theory of human development.

In 1901, in the early days of the progressive movement, Hall gave what Charles Strickland and Charles Burgess have called his single most important pronouncement on education. Speaking at the NEA convention, Hall presented a paper entitled "The Ideal School as Based on Child Study." He described his school as "pediocentric" (child-centered). Instead of fitting the child to the school, Hall wanted teachers to fit the school to the child. In the ideal school, the child would develop naturally, while the teacher kept "out of nature's way," defending "the happiness and rights of children." Hall's conception of the child as a plant, with the teacher as a kind of gardener who protects him from harm while allowing him to grow and develop according to his nature, is not unlike that of Friedrich Froebel, the German educator who originated the kindergarten—"the children garden." Hall recognized Froebel as one of the "deepest of all modern educational thinkers."

Although Hall found himself in agreement with Froebel, he found others who disagreed with him. For many

Americans, including Hall's former teacher, William James, the recapitulation conception of human development smacked too much of determinism. James, a staunch opponent of determinism, propounded an entirely different conception of human development, yet one still within the framework of evolution. He saw man as a free agent interacting with his environment. Out of this interaction between the self and the environment, one develops habits, which James called "the flywheel of human behavior." By the time we reach adult life, according to James, "ninety-nine hundredths, or, possibly, nine hundred and ninety-nine thousandths of our activity is purely automatic and habitual." Man is nothing more than a "walking bundle of habits."

As early as 1892 James had urged teachers to use the findings of the psychologists, "which may enable you to labor more easily and effectively in the several schoolrooms over which you preside." In his *Talks to Teachers* he insisted that "the teacher's supreme concern should be to ingrain into the pupil that assortment of habits that should be most useful to him throughout life." In James' theory of instruction then, we find that the teacher does not, as Hall proposed, stand aside and allow matters to take their course. Instead, the teacher must select those habits she wants the child to acquire, and then proceed to "ingrain them into the pupil." James' theory of human development was not based upon any empirical procedures; thus, he never determined just how habits came into being. This empirical task was carried on by another of his famous pupils, Edward Lee Thorndike.

Taking James' view of habits as the result of the interaction between the self and the environment, Thorndike tried to search out the scientific laws that accounted for this phenomenon. Using a "problem-box" and a supply of chickens, cats, and other small animals, Thorndike discovered that after a series of trials a boxed animal more quickly pressed the lever that released him from the problem-box. He called this "learning." At this point Thorndike used the term "situation" and "response" to describe the interaction of the self with its environment. The environment or situation (e.g., trapped in a "problem-box") calls forth a response from the organism (e.g., stepping on the lever that opens the door). When a specific response becomes "wedded" to a specific situation, when, that is, the same situation always calls forth the same response from the organism, then we can say that learning has taken place. We might use James' term and say that a habit has been formed; or, in Thorndike's terminology, we might say that the organism has become conditioned. After looking at interaction in terms of situation-response, Thorndike was able to discover the laws that explained how a specific response became wedded or connected to a specific situation. One of the most famous of these laws of learning is "the law of effect" according to which responses that are *rewarded* are "stamped in."

Thorndike, like James, had the teacher deciding what habits or connections to ingrain into the students. He had developed a fairly sophisticated theory of instruction, but it was not the theory the progressives were looking for. In spite of the fact that Thorndike and James looked at the child as an evolving organism, and the teacher as an agent to maximize that evolution or development, the role they gave the teacher was too authoritative for the progressives. The progressives did not want the teacher to supply a set of fixed goals for the students. They wanted the teacher to bring out the potential talents of each student, no matter what these might be. The work of James and Thorndike merely provided a psychological theory of instruction that gave support to the old ways of training, molding, and forming children according to some set of fixed aims.

On the other hand, Hall's theory of instruction was no more acceptable to the progressives because of its implicit determinism. According to Hall the child will—if left alone and protected by the teacher—naturally realize his fullest development. But one could never be sure that this would, in fact, occur. The progressives wanted a theory of instruction that had the teacher guide and direct the development of the child, without, at the same time, imposing his goals on that child's growth. John Dewey provided just such a theory.

VIII

Like both James and Thorndike, John Dewey saw human development, or growth, in terms of the interaction between the self and the environment. This interaction he called "experience." He cautioned, however, that not all experience contributes to growth, or, put another way, not all experience is educative. Educative, or growth-producing, experiences are those that alter our traditional patterns of behavior in such a way that we are better able to function in the world in which we live.

Dewey viewed man as a goal-seeking organism. Man acts purposefully. So long as he is behaving rationally, man's behavior is directed toward some "end-in-view." The environment sustains this behavior, or this activity. Thus, one is able to walk to the store to buy a pack of cigarettes because there is a sidewalk to walk on, traffic lights to permit crossing streets, a store supplied with cigarettes, and so forth. However, the environment not only sustains activity, it sometimes frustrates or hinders pursuit of the end-in-view. The store, for example, might be out of cigarettes or out of one's brand of cigarettes. When the environment presents us with obstacles, hindrances, or frustrations, we have the initial and necessary conditions for growth or development. People, Dewey insisted, grow or develop only when they are confronted with problems, or have what he called "felt difficulties." In trying to overcome a difficulty, hindrance, or problem, man must alter his traditional behavior. Sometimes he must develop new ways of behaving. If the new behavior overcomes the difficulty and solves the problem, then we can say that the organism has developed, has grown.

There are, Dewey said, definite steps the organism takes in creating new ways of behavior. These steps are no less than the scientific method. Man grows through making experiments. Like a scientist, man encounters problems, formulates hypotheses, and tests them. When the hypothesis works out in practice, when it is confirmed, then the problem is solved, the difficulties overcome. Thus, when I discover that the store is out of cigarettes I might buy a cigar, look for another store, or try a new brand. Each of these suggestions can serve as an hypothesis that I could test. In this case the test would be: does this way of behaving satisfy the need I feel for my usual brand of cigarettes? If none of these hypotheses meets the test, I keep searching for one that does. When I discover a hypothesis that works out, then I have developed a way of behaving that will be appropriate whenever I again encounter the same problem. Or I might even become a cigar smoker, or a steady customer of another store, or make some other new radical change in my traditional behavior. Whatever course of action I take, if I solve my problem, then I have furthered my ability to cope with, or function in, the world in which I live.

This theory of human development provided Dewey with the basis for a theory of instruction in which the teachers could guide and direct the growth of a child without imposing his own goals on the child's growth. The teacher's primary task is to supply the child with problems, the initial and necessary conditions for growth. The teacher must exercise care in selecting the problems since they must be the *child's* problems, not the teacher's. So the problems must consist of obstacles to the pupil's own ends-in-view. Moreover, care must be taken to ensure that the child is ready to confront the problem—ready psychologically, physiologically, and intellectually. When possible the problems should not be totally novel, but should have some connection to, or continuity with, the child's past experiences. Finally, if an experience is to be truly educative the teacher must pay attention to the quality of the experience. That is, the experience must not be a disagreeable one that might repel the student, and at the same time it must be an effective experience, one that "will live fruitfully and creatively in subsequent experience."

For Dewey there were no "ends" or "goals" in education; nothing fixed and determinate. Education was growth, and growth was a process with no end, or goal, save further growth. The teacher had the job of maximizing the possibilities for growth, both present and future, by supplying the child with *real* problems, helping him to formulate hypotheses and guiding him in testing them. In this way the child learned how to learn—he learned the scientific method of discovery.

Dewey's theory of instruction became the instructional theory of the progressives. By taking the growth of the child as his central concern and by analyzing the process of growth itself in terms of the scientific method, Dewey provided a theory of instruction that liberated the child, and still provided a crucial, guiding role for the teacher.

John Dewey went further. He gave the progressives a theory of education as well as a theory of instruction, a theory of education that cast the school into the role of model for a truly participant democracy. In the schools, Dewey admitted, the child may acquire technical, specialized ability in algebra, Latin, or botany. But if this is mere "isolated intellectual learning," then the school contradicts its own aim. Its aim is to educate the child, but unless the child understands "the meaning which things have in life of which he is a part," he is not educated, he is merely trained. Students, Dewey said, had to acquire the "social sense" or the "social direction" of the "disposition acquired." One way to do this, he suggested, was to engage in joint activities that call these technical abilities into play. Therefore, the problems the teacher confronts his students with should be *shared problems* that will generate this joint activity. These shared problems must be "real" problems; that is, problems that "reflect the life of the larger society." This makes the school an embryonic community, in which the child is saturated "with the spirit of service," and provided "with the instruments of effective self-direction." In this way, Dewey concludes, "we shall have the deepest and best guarantee of a larger society which is worthy, lovely, and harmonious."

For Dewey then the school was to be the model for the larger society precisely because democracy, participant democracy, is nothing more than people engaging in joint

activity to solve their common or shared problems. With
Dewey progressive political theory became one with progressive educational theory. Democracy for him was more
than a form of government; it was a way of life, and
children would learn that way of life in the American
schools.

IX

John Dewey's educational theory
clearly exposes the epistemological differences between
the earlier liberal reformers and the progressives. The
liberal reformers were pessimists. They had lost faith in
the ability of the masses to know the truth, much less
to use it as a guide to action. So they designed an educational program to produce both an elite who would
lead and a disciplined mass that would willingly accept
the rational, virtuous leadership of that elite.
The progressives, in contrast, were epistemological
optimists. They believed that all men could perceive the
truth once it was made manifest. Moreover, they believed that all men would use this truth as a guide to
action. The progressives' educational program, Dewey's
version of it, envisions a society wherein all citizens are
nothing less than scientists, working together and jointly
solving their common problems.

The same optimism is reflected in higher education
during the progressive era. The liberal reformers had
looked to colleges and universities to supply a cadre of
leaders. Through civil service examinations these college
graduates were to gain access to positions of political
power. The progressive, in contrast, stressed the power of
ideas, rather than the power of men. They showed less
enthusiasm for civil service reform, concentrating in-

stead on developing ways of releasing and promulgating information, facts, knowledge, and ideas to the masses. The best example of a progressive university during this period was the University of Wisconsin. Here, Charles Van Hise, who served as president from 1903 to 1918, declared that he expected the university to "carry out knowledge to the people."

At Wisconsin a vast network of agencies came into being to perform this task of carrying knowledge to the people. Correspondence courses were established in all fields of study. And to supplement this the university conducted college extension classes throughout the state. In addition, it set up institutes, held conferences, promoted lectures, and designed exhibits to educate all people in all places "for the daily occupations of life." Perhaps the creation of the Department of General Information and Welfare expresses best the service function the university had now adopted. This was a clearinghouse of almost any kind of service or information, serving individuals, clubs, cities, counties, or commercial organizations. Frederick Howe described it as the "questions and answers department of the state."

While the liberal reformers had looked to the colleges and universities to supply leaders, or even experts, the progressives now looked to them for consultants. Unlike leaders and experts, consultants make no policy decisions; they only advise. During this period the University of Wisconsin provided a host of advisers and consultants. By 1908, for example, forty-one members of the faculty were serving as members of one or more state commissions. In fact, Van Hise and one of his deans each sat on five state commissions. Many have referred to the University of Wisconsin of this period as "the fourth branch of government." What this quip distorts is the important though obvious fact that the university had no intention of becoming an official branch of the state government, nor did its faculty want to get into political offices. The job of the university was to reveal the truth —to the politicians as well as the people. And so long as those in office were open and ready to receive the truth, it did not make too much difference who they were or what political party they represented.

X

The First World War broke the back of political progressivism. Robert La Follette had argued against American entry into the war, predicting that this would "set progress back a generation." Even Woodrow Wilson, when he finally decided that America must enter the conflict, did so with forebodings of gloom. The night before he asked Congress to declare war, he confided to newspaperman Frank Cobb: "To fight you must be brutal and ruthless, and the spirit of ruthless brutality will enter into the very fiber of our national life, infecting Congress, the courts, the policeman on the beat, the man in the street."

Knowing that the progressive impulse was rooted in a humanitarian concern for others, Wilson tried to preserve these humanitarian feelings by couching the entry into the war, and the later peace negotiations, in the language and rhetoric of the progressive movement itself. He explained intervention in lofty phrases, using moral terms to justify America's role—tying it to altruism and to self-sacrifice. America was opening a crusade to make the world safe for democracy. But, as Hofstadter has observed, by linking the war to progressive rhetoric and progressive values, Wilson unintentionally ensured that the American people would repudiate progressivism, when they ultimately, but inevitably, repudiated the war.

During the twenties, Americans euphemistically referred to their repudiation of the war as "the return to normalcy." At this point hedonism replaced the spirit of self-sacrifice, the sense of responsibility gave way to neglect, and civic participation disappeared in the face of widespread apathy. Progressivism was dead. The participant democracy the progressives had hoped to create never materialized. During the twenties the initiative, the referendum, and recall were invoked sparingly. Moreover, when the practices introduced by the progressives were actually used, they produced little change in the political or economic situation. Female suffrage made no appreciable difference nor did the direct election of senators. And the direct primary left nominations where they had always been, in the hands of party managers. Summarizing the impact of progressivism on the twenties, Eric Goldman has concluded that "the most conspicuous result was the lack of any result."

In the twenties American intellectuals bade farewell to reform, losing all hopes of creating a participant democratic society. To many, reform and democracy seemed incompatible. After all it was a democratic society that now tolerated the Ku Klux Klan, jailed Sacco and Vanzetti, staged the Scopes Trial, and imposed a nationwide prohibition on alcoholic beverages. Henry L. Mencken, one of the heroes of the age, declared that democracy in the end came to nothing but the mob, which was "sodden, brutal, and ignorant." Mencken made interest in social questions ludicrous and unfashionable. Democracy became a farce. "All the known facts lie flatly against it." It was he who wrote, "I enjoy democracy enormously. It is incomparably idiotic, and hence incomparably amusing." Mencken stirred up violent opposition, but not against his political satire. Few cared. "It was characteristic of the Jazz Age," said F. Scott Fitzgerald, "that it had no interest in politics at all."

During this apolitical period, a group of educators in 1919 founded an organization they named the Progressive Education Association (PEA). Ignoring the union between political and educational progressivism that John Dewey had forged a few years earlier in *Democracy and Education*, the leaders of this new association set out to impose the dogma of child-centered pedagogy on American educational reform. The Progressive Education Association ignored the political function of the schools, disregarding thereby the fact that American educational reform had come into being as an integral part of American political reforms. Nothing better illustrates how oblivious these educators were to this than their choice of Charles W. Eliot as the first honorary president of the PEA. Significantly, John Dewey refused to join. After the death of Eliot in 1926, he finally did accept the honorary presidency.

According to Stanwood Cobb, the first executive secretary, the early members of the PEA "aimed at nothing short of reforming the entire school system of America." But as Lawrence Cremin has noted, "one looks in vain for the reformism that had been the leitmotif of the movement before 1919." Severed from its connection with political progressivism, progressive education lost its momentum as a reform movement, becoming merely a pedagogical attitude. The editor of *Progressive Education*, writing about the 1926 conference of the PEA, reported that "each speaker had his own intimate message and no two would agree on the ramifications of technique. Yet all were invested and animated with an inquisitive attitude, a searching for the best way to enrich and to cultivate the essence of children. . . . Progressive education can never formulate more than an inquisitive attitude. Each child is a law unto himself."

During the twenties the main work of the PEA was in the area of "creative expression." *Progressive Education* devoted a number of special issues to this theme in the fields of art, literature, music, and dramatics. "Creative expression" was the central theme of the decade's most representative educational book, *The Child-Centered School*, written by Harold Rugg and Ann Shumaker. In the child-centered school, they exclaimed, "the lid of restraint is being lifted from the child in order that he may come to his own best self fulfillment." "The new school," they wrote,

> assumes that every child is endowed with the capacity to express himself, and that this innate capacity is immensely worth cultivating. The pupil is placed in an atmosphere conducive to self-expression in every aspect. Some will create with words, others with light. Some will express themselves through the body in the dance; others will model, carve, shape their idea in plastic materials. Still others will find expression through oral languages, and some through an integrated physical, emotional dramatic gesture. But whatever the route, the medium, the materials—each one has some capacity for expression.

The authors of *The Child-Centered School* related this child-centered education to John Dewey's concept of growth. They thought that this concept "cut through the crust of the disciplinary conception of education," uncovering what they took to be the most crucial question of all: "How shall the activities and materials of instruction be organized to guarantee maximum child growth?"

Rugg and Shumaker were not alone in finding a rationale for child-centered education in John Dewey's theory of instruction. And like the others who bolstered "creative expression" by references to Dewey's conception of growth, they ignored his *theory of education* which made the growth of the individual the means to create a community, a participant democracy. These "progressive" educators of the apolitical twenties showed little concern for this side of John Dewey. As Rugg himself later confessed, they were "radical in educational method . . . but not in social philosophy." Then, after 1929, things began to change. After 1929 those who called themselves "progressive" educators could no longer ignore the social realities in America.

XI

"I have no fears for the future of our country," Herbert Hoover intoned in his inaugural address in March 1929. "It is bright with hope." Seven months later the stock market crashed, following which America entered the worst depression of its history. As wage cuts and unemployment increased, the people sank into an abyss of despair.

The Depression dispelled the apolitical outlook of the twenties. Something had to be done to revive the nation, and the government seemed to be the only agency powerful enough to do this. As the elections of 1932 approached, people looked for a candidate who could solve the economic crisis. The Democrats found a leader in Franklin D. Roosevelt. In his acceptance speech he told the people just what they longed to hear. The American people, he said, wanted two things, "work, with all the moral and spiritual values that go with it; and with work, a reasonable measure of security—security for themselves and for their wives and children." Then, before a roaring convention throng he declared "I pledge you—I pledge myself to a new deal for the American people."

To give the people work and security, "a New Deal," the powers and functions of the government had to be expanded. Roosevelt proceeded to expand and strengthen federal control over banks and railroads, security issues and security exchanges, public utility holding companies, motor carriers, and industrial and agricultural production. Under Roosevelt the federal government for the first time forbade employers to interfere with their employees' right to organize and engage in collective bargaining. It established minimum wages, maximum hours, and child-labor regulations.

In addition to expanding its regulatory functions, the federal government now began to provide extensive services for citizens: jobs for the needy and unemployed, housing for lower income families, cheap electric power, and loans to farmers and homeowners, as well as to banks and railroads.

As a reform movement the New Deal stood squarely in the tradition of political progressivism; indeed, it made the work of the progressives seem timid by comparison. Nevertheless, the New Deal represented a departure from the progressive tradition. And in departing from the progressives, the New Deal broke with American tradition. For, insofar as the progressives had fought against privilege and monopoly in an attempt to give the small man a better chance, they were in the general American tradition of democratic reformers. They had differed from the earlier American reformers (e.g., the liberal reformers), since they had given a positive role to the government, whereas traditionally the strategy of reform had been to constrict or curtail the activity of the government in the economic sector. In granting the government a positive role, however, the progressives had viewed that role as a preventive one, or a regulatory one.

With the New Deal this preventive role of the government gave way to the role of protector of all the people. The government now had the task of providing security for all, to prevent them from any and all hazards—unemployment, accident, illness, old age, and death. Equally important was the thrust of the New Deal—it came from the top. Unlike the progressives, the New Dealers had no concern with bringing about a participant democracy, they did not crusade to "restore government to the people." The New Deal, in Richard Hofstadter's words, was a "managerial reorganization of society." Most Americans accepted this thrust from the top, this governmental organization of society. Their traditional fear of government tyranny gave way to the greater fear for their own welfare and security—freedom from government seemed much less important than freedom from want.

Franklin Roosevelt had no master plan. The New Deal did not represent economic planning so much as "a chaos of experimentation." Roosevelt had in 1932 prescribed "bold persistent experimentation," explaining that he thought it was "common sense to take a method and try it. If it fails, admit it frankly and try another." He defended this drive to do something with the warning that the people would not "stand by silently forever while the things to satisfy their needs are within easy reach."

His role, the role of the government, was to do something about those needs of the people—farmers who needed markets, unemployed who needed jobs, the hungry who needed food, the banks that needed money, and so on. Roosevelt was not a philosopher, nor did the New Deal and its program of social welfare emerge from a political theory. The New Deal rested on a point of view —meeting the needs of the people. It was an opportunistic point of view, one that suited practical politicians, administrators, technicians—men who wanted to get things done.

The needs of one group of people attracted the particular attention of the New Deal: American youth. Those between the ages of sixteen and twenty-four made up the largest number of all unemployed in the nation. Between 1929 and 1935 the number of all unemployed youth increased by about 30 percent. Most American youths needed jobs but could find none; some needed further education, but could not afford it. What were they to do? Or rather what could be done for them? Could their needs be met?

One attempt to meet the needs of youth was the Civilian Conservation Corps (CCC) which Roosevelt established within three months after taking office. This program employed youths to perform useful public work —planting trees, restoring streams, protecting wildlife, fighting dust storms. Housed in camps built and managed by the war department, they were able to send home to their families a good part of their dollar-a-day wages.

To further reduce unemployment the New Deal set up the National Youth Administration (NYA) in 1935. This program kept youth out of the competition for regular jobs by creating new part-time public service jobs that permitted them to continue their schooling. Through this program thousands were able to pay their way through college and over a million able to stay in high school.

XII

And what about the schools? If America in the thirties had a "youth problem," were the schools able to cope with it? Could the schools help to meet the needs of youth? Many thought not. The American Council on Education, for example, organized an American Youth Commission in 1935 with the declaration: "Recent social and economic changes in the United States have given rise to difficulties in the care and education of young people with which existing institutions are quite unprepared to deal adequately."

Earlier, at the 1932 convention of the PEA, George S. Counts had challenged the child-centered doctrine that continued to dominate American educational practice. At that meeting in an address entitled, "Dare Progressive Education Be Progressive?" Counts urged the members to focus more on the society, less on the child. He dared them to "face squarely and courageously every social issue, come to grips with life in all its stark reality, establish an organic relation with the community, develop a realistic and comprehensive theory of welfare, fashion a compelling and challenging vision of human destiny. . . ." He wanted them not only to become society-centered, but actually to reconstruct American society. Dismissing as "bogeys" the fears of *imposition* and *indoctrination*, Counts proclaimed that competition must give way to cooperation, the urge for profits to careful planning, and private capitalism to some form of socialized economy.

In his speech Counts was expressing a position that had been developing among his colleagues at Teachers

College, Columbia University. In 1933, one of them, William Heard Kilpatrick, edited a book of position papers under the title *The Educational Frontier*. This volume contained articles that expressed deep concern about socioeconomic conditions in America and a plea for educators to confront them. As if to explain what Counts had meant in his earlier address when he had dismissed the fears of indoctrination, Kilpatrick now wrote: "If to prepare individuals to take part intelligently in the management of conditions under which they will live, to bring them to an understanding of the forces which are moving, to equip them with the intellectual and practical tools by which they can themselves enter into direction of these forces, is indoctrination, then the philosophy of education which we have in mind may be adjudged to be an instrument of indoctrination."

The notions of these social reformers found expression in two further ventures: *The Social Frontier*, a journal first published at Teachers College in 1934, and the John Dewey Society for the Study of Education and Culture, organized in 1935. The John Dewey Society published its first yearbook, *The Teacher and Society*, in 1937. Kilpatrick, who edited it, explained that it was devoted to the study of the teacher in relation to society because "under existing conditions the teacher is the crucial factor in any conscious effort to bring school and society effectively together." The book contained a number of different articles dealing, in Kilpatrick's words, with the "various phases of the problem in such a way as to help both teacher and teaching serve more vitally the cause of a better society."

The movement to use teachers and the schools as the lever to reconstruct the society never gained much headway among American schoolmen. But whether it was the pressing reality of the youth problem or the work of men like Counts and Kilpatrick, most educators during the thirties did shift the focus of concern away from the child to the youth. Most educational discussions now attended to the secondary level of education. Moreover, these discussions went beyond the psychological concerns of the child-centered twenties to include appraisals of the social context.

The best illustration of this shift of pedagogical concern is the work of the Commission on Secondary School Curriculum. This commission, created by the PEA, published its most important report in 1934, *Reorganizing Secondary Education*. In it, the commission adopted an approach to schooling that soon dominated all educational literature. It reorganized the curriculum around "the needs of youth."

Rather than reconstruct the society, these investigators wanted teachers to recognize and to meet both the personal, or psychological, needs of their students and their social needs. The members of the commission took the psychological needs to be those demands society makes on the individual. They insisted that "a working concept of an educational need must always be both personal and social in reference; it must always incorporate both the present desires of the individual and what they should desirably become." The commission was not the first to suggest basing the curriculum on the needs of youth. Keaton and Koopman had published *A College Curriculum Based on Functional Needs of Students* in 1936. And the year before Goodwin Watson had delivered an address at the NEA convention, entitled, "Problems of Youth—What Does Youth Most Need?" But in *Reorganizing Secondary Education*, the Commission on Secondary School Curriculum did provide the most comprehensive and far-reaching program for curriculum reform. The commission organized the resources of six fields (science, social studies, mathematics, language, literature, and art) into four basic areas: immediate personal-social relationships, social-civic relationships, economic relationships, and personal living. Each of these "basic areas" was further analyzed in terms of "needs," to guide the reorganization of the secondary schools. For example, the needs identified under economic relationships were: (1) the need for emotional assurance of progress toward adult status; (2) the need for guidance in choosing an occupation and for vocational preparation; (3) the need for wise selection and use of goods and services; and (4) the need for effective action in solving basic economic problems.

Of course, the American secondary schools never adopted the entire reorganization plan of the commission, but the concept of meeting the needs of youth soon became the basis for all educational planning. By 1942 Donald C. Doane could write in his published doctoral dissertation: "If there is one point upon which most educators today appear to be in agreement it is that educational programs, particularly those of the secondary school, should be founded upon the needs of the children concerned." This work, *The Needs of Youth: An Evaluation for Curriculum Proposals*, was an attempt to analyze and classify the many different opinions "as to just what these needs are and what they imply for the curriculum."

Despite the efforts of Doane, no agreement was reached by American educators as to what the needs of youth were. As a result the concept of need lent support to a rapidly expanding curriculum. In 1934 there was almost double the 68 subjects offered a mere twelve years earlier. By 1944, according to John F. Latimer, one could find 141 different subjects in the high school curriculum. But more significant than the numerical increase was the shift in the quality of the curriculum. As late as 1934 the leading fields of study in the high schools were foreign languages, mathematics, and science. By 1949 more students were studying health, music, and art than any other fields. By this time more than half the subjects in the curriculum were in the fields of social studies, vocational education, home economics, and agriculture, and student concentration in these fields was almost as great as the concentration in the fields of foreign language, mathematics, science and English.

In the fifties, as we shall see, the scope and the quality of the high school curriculum came under violent attack. Most of these attacks came from outside the profession, but within the profession itself the concept of need came under searching analytic scrutiny. In " 'Need' and the Needs-Curriculum," B. Paul Komisar showed the triviality, the vagueness, and the indeterminacy of the concept of need and its total inadequacy as a basis for making educational policy.

Still, the concept of need and the needs curriculum had brought to the fore the welfare function of the American school. In keeping with the point of view of the New Deal, the schools, like the government, had the task of caring for the needs of people. And perhaps more important than the emergence of this function was the new relationship it created between the schools and the state. The schools now came to be regarded as a part of the government itself. The schools were one of the agencies of welfare—agencies of the state. So just as the New Deal made a radical break with the tradition of American political reform, so also the schools of the period made a radical break with their traditional political function.

Traditionally, the American schools were societal institutions, not state or governmental ones. Politically they functioned to protect society from the possible evils that the government might perpetrate. Even the progressives had looked to the schools as the agency to protect society from governmental tyranny. But now in the thirties, the schools, for the first time, came to be regarded as one of the governmental agencies functioning to cure the ills and the evils of society and to improve the general welfare. Of course the American schools had always had the job of improving the general welfare, but this had been a social function. From now on it was to be a political function.

XIII

One hundred and fifty years ago Thomas Jefferson wrote: "If a nation expects to be ignorant and free, in a state of civilization, it expects what never was, and never will be." When Lyndon B. Johnson delivered his State of the Union address in January 1965, he revealed the profound change that had taken place in America when he announced: "Thomas Jefferson said no nation can be both ignorant and free. Today no nation can be both ignorant and great."

In the 1960's Americans seemed less concerned with freedom than with greatness. They would have, in President Johnson's words, a "Great Society." Yet, it would not be accurate to say that they were less concerned with freedom than heretofore; it was just that Americans no longer regarded their own government as a threat to their freedom. The New Deal, the Second World War, and the Cold War had all fostered the growth of government and governmental power. By the sixties, the traditional

Jeffersonian distinction between the society and the state was disappearing as governmental control over society increased. By this time, as Daniel Bell has written, the United States had become a *national society*. Now "all crucial political and economic decisions" were made by the government, creating a national economy and a national polity. The state, in short, directed social change.

This expanded governmental power had not produced government tyranny. Indeed, the expanded powers of the government had raised the general welfare of the society, giving the people social security against those who threatened "the American way of life."

By the sixties most Americans not only no longer feared governmental tyranny, they felt that only the government could guarantee the blessings they enjoyed. Above all, only the government could secure the nation against those foreign powers that threatened to "enslave" America.

The only way to be secure was to be powerful, to be great, greater than any other nation. In the late fifties, John F. Kennedy could base his successful campaign for the Presidency largely on the warning that the United States was in danger of losing its hegemony. Lamenting the missile gap, the declining rate of economic growth, and the loss of prestige abroad, he promised to "get the country moving again." Kennedy's New Frontier led, naturally, to Johnson's Great Society.

To create this Great Society President Johnson turned to the schools. In July 1964, he said: "If we are learning anything from our experiences, we are learning that it is time for us to go to work, and the first work of these times and the first work of our society is education." Johnson, a former schoolteacher, confessed that he would like to be remembered as the "education President." Yet he was not the first Cold War executive to give such high priority to education. Back in 1949 President Harry S Truman had said, "Education is our first line of defense." He went on to add, "In the conflict of principle which divides the world today, America's hope, our hope, the hope of the world is in education. . . . Education is the most important task before us."

Truman, like most, saw the conflict with the Communist nations as an ideological one. The educational task then consisted of instructing all in the knowledge of good and evil; that is, all people—both at home and abroad—must learn to recognize the virtues of democratic capitalism and the evils of communism. This ideological conception of the Cold War continued into the fifties. It was how the Educational Policies Commission saw things in its 1951 report, *Education and National Security*. After describing the world that Americans then faced, the report announced that there was a moral task to be performed. Regretting the "profound misunderstanding of the meaning of America in most parts of the world—and among some Americans," it declared that "we must come to know ourselves" and to others "we must make clear our devotion to moral purposes." Turning to the role of the school, the members of the commission found little to disturb them in the emphases and programs of the schools. Above all, they insisted, "the schools must educate for moral and spiritual values," since "the problems which now most urgently require solution are not physical or technical, but moral and social."

What worried the commission most, as it did most concerned observers, was the matter of staffing and financing the schools of the nation. During the Second World War many teachers had left the classroom, and now with the war babies beginning to enter the schools, the nation faced a severe teacher shortage. Moreover, the increased school population necessitated increased expenditures for new buildings and new equipment. The need for money was dire indeed, and the Educational Policies Commission merely reflected a widely held opinion when it declared: "if we dedicate to our schools sufficient funds to operate them well, we shall have taken important steps to safeguard our future."

Inevitably, the requests for money for school equipment, school buildings, and schoolteachers brought forth angry opposition from many taxpayers. The American principle of local control of the schools gave homeowners the opportunity to express their dissatisfaction with the rapid inflation of the postwar years. And express it they did as time and time again proposed school bonds went down in defeat at the polls. In their fight to prevent new expenditures, these tax-conscious citizens turned a critical eye toward the current ones. Here they discovered, predictably, that much of their tax money was being spent on "fads and frills" and "costly palaces." They also uncovered teachers who defended the fads and frills, but who couldn't teach Johnny to read. The criticisms frequently extended to the teacher-training institutions, the schools of education that foisted such ill-prepared teachers on an innocent public. Viewing them as part of the establishment that conspired to control teacher certification, the public affected shock and dismay at revelations that Einstein could not be hired to teach science in the schools of many states, nor Beethoven to teach music. They, you see, had not taken enough credits in "methods courses" in a school of education.

This searching reappraisal of American education led, in 1956, to a White House Conference on Education.

The delegates to this conference identified the most urgent problems facing the American schools. The first problem was one of objectives. But the remaining ones all centered about the issues of staffing, equipping, and building. Of greatest importance, according to the conference report, was the problem of public interest and support.

During the very year of the White House Conference on Education some Americans began to see the role of the schools in a new light. In April, William Benton, one-time United States Senator, reported the following in *The New York Times Magazine*: "A recent trip to the USSR has convinced me that education has become a main feature of the cold war; that Russia's classrooms and libraries, her laboratories and teaching methods may threaten us more than her hydrogen bombs."

The Senator seemed to be right, for when in October of the following year Americans witnessed the first Russian sputnik, they attributed this feat to the superior schooling provided in the USSR. The chancellor of the University of Kansas, for example, in an address before the American Council on Education six months after the Russian triumph declared: "The message which this little ball carries to Americans, if they would but stop and listen, is that in the last half of the twentieth century . . . nothing is as important as the trained and educated mind. This sphere tells us not of the desirability, but of the utmost necessity of the highest quality and expanded dimensions of the educational effort."

The message was clear. While the schools in the United States had concentrated on ideology, the Soviets had stressed quality instruction in basic subjects. Technological supremacy was the payoff. And the Russians had won the first round.

So now Americans must have quality education. Admiral Hyman Rickover, the "father" of the atomic submarine, in his best-selling book on American education announced: "Now that we have been aroused to the dangerous effect which poor education has on our strength and influence as a world power, let not men of little vision with their soothing words hold back our righteous anger. We must sweep clean the temple of learning and bring back quality."

Some educators tried to defend the American school system on the grounds that it served the needs of *all* people and did not cater to an elite of gifted students as was the case in Europe and in the USSR. But the American public was in no mood for this kind of argument. John Gardner, who wrote "Pursuit of Excellence," the Rockefeller Report on Education, answered in the form of an ultimatum: "From time to time one still hears arguments over *quantity* versus *quality* education. Behind such arguments is the assumption that a society can choose to educate a few people exceedingly well, *or* to educate a great number of people somewhat less well, but that it cannot do both. But a modern society such as ours cannot choose to do one *or* the other. It has no choice but to do both."

The infusion of quality into American education now came to be one of the primary concerns of the federal government. The first move was the passage of the 1958 National Defense Education Act. This set up institutes to upgrade teachers of foreign languages, mathematics, and science, and provided improved guidance programs to urge more students to become linguists, scientists, and mathematicians. During the next seven years the federal government expanded this initial narrow outlook to a concern for the *total quality* of American education. Since 1958 it has passed the Higher Education Facilities Act, the Library Services Act, the Vocational and Technical Education Act, the Nurses Training Act, the Economic Opportunity Act, the Civil Rights Act, the Higher Education Act, the Federal Arts and Humanities Foundation Act, and the International Education Act. And when Congress renewed the National Defense Education Act it broadened the number of different fields of study included in its benefits. The culmination of this landslide of educational legislation was the Elementary and Secondary Education Act of 1965—"An Act to strengthen and improve educational quality and educational opportunities in the Nation's elementary and secondary schools."

XIV

When Congress passed the Elementary and Secondary Education Act of 1965, President Johnson declared that it was "the greatest breakthrough in the advance of education since the Constitution was written." Whether or not it advanced education, this act did culminate *the* greatest federal breakthrough into American education.

By supplying all American schools with money—a total commitment of over $4 billion for 1965 alone—the government had guaranteed that they would be agencies of the state—agencies of national defense, or national security, or national welfare.

The federal breakthrough penetrated most deeply into higher education, where it had begun long before sputnik. During the Second World War the government had turned to scientists in the laboratories of universities throughout the country for technical assistance. This cooperation continued into the period of the Cold War, leading, during the Eisenhower Administration, to the creation of the National Science Foundation to support university research and to pay for the training of researchers. This twenty-year or so period of common-law marriage between the states and institutions of higher learning produced what Clark Kerr termed a transformation of the university. In his remarkable Godkin lectures of 1963 he described the results of this transformation: the "multiversity"—a federal grant university that served as "a prime instrument of national purpose." By 1960, Kerr reported, the federal government had given about $1.5 billion to higher education. Of this, $1 billion was for research, and this accounted for 75 percent of all university expenditures on research. "Clearly," he concluded, "the shape and nature of university research are profoundly affected by federal monies."

This *statification* of the universities did more than affect the shape and nature of university research. As Kerr himself noted, the university's control over its own destiny had been substantially reduced. Moreover, the individual scholar, by engaging in the negotiations for federal funds, reduced the authority of the department chairmen, deans, and the president. Understandably the schools had already been used to help meet the successive challenges of Depression, hot war, and Cold War. But now more than ever before, they were mobilized, or ready to be mobilized, *by the government* to meet *national* needs. Many faculty members now shifted their loyalties from their university to Washington, D.C. This transformation also included a great shift in emphasis within the universities—toward the physical sciences, the biomedical sciences and engineering, and away from the humanities and social sciences. Not only the balance among the fields, but the balance among institutions also changed, since federal grants concentrated research at certain universities.

Finally, this transformation greatly reduced the quality of undergraduate instruction as professors spent more and more time on their research projects with graduate students. Most observers point to this as the underlying cause for the 1964 undergraduate revolution at the University of California—Clark Kerr's own university. Kerr, earlier in his Godkin lectures, had neither approved nor defended the transformed university; he merely analyzed and described "the wave of the future." The implication, however, was that all realistic people must bow and accept it, like it or not. The students at Berkeley, however, refused to concur. Their revolt set off a torrent of commentaries and analyses from academics, some filled with admonitions for the student protesters, but many more filled with self-incriminating praise for them.

By 1965 Americans had abandoned their traditional fear of their own government. The consensus among most Americans was that in acting on behalf of what was called the national interest, their government was acting on behalf of them and society. Many now expected the schools to engineer and to perpetuate this consensus.

SIX ‖ CONCLUSION

The Americans' faith in their schools goes back to the beginnings. In their new land the early settlers looked to the schools to preserve civilization. Later generations looked to the schools to prepare youth for the unexpected job in this land of opportunity. Still later, when the Americans created the first new nation, they looked to the schools to perform a political function, to ensure the success of republican government.

Ostensibly the schools succeeded; civilization was preserved, the economy expanded, and the republic secured. But as the work of Bernard Bailyn and Rush Welter has revealed, there was a host of informal agencies of education that played perhaps a more important role in these tasks. Probably the very vastness of the land, the diffuseness of its people and institutions helped hide from the Americans the fact that their schools were not the primary or sole agency of civilization, not the primary or sole vocational training agency, not the primary or sole agency of politicalization. But the problems had been solved, and most Americans did attribute success to the schools.

After the Civil War the nation gave the school even more complex responsibilities. The school was to become the panacea for all social problems. I have tried to show that the school failed to solve the multiple problems generated by urbanization, industrialization, emancipation, and nationalization. Moreover, in some cases this faith in the power of the schools actually aggravated these problems. Rather than bring about a racially integrated society, the schools reinforced segregation; rather than educate people to cope with life in the city, they accelerated the flight from the city and aided in the spread of urban blight. By 1965 the schools had polarized American society into self-satisfied whites and victimized blacks, into despondent city dwellers and indifferent suburbanites.

In their attempts to cope with industrialization by providing equality of opportunity in the success race, the schools once again polarized the society by identifying, indeed creating, the winners and the losers. And with regard to their political function the schools by 1965 had completely reversed themselves, moving from the original role of preventing governmental tyranny to become a primary agency of the state in its pursuit of the national purpose. Once again the result was polarization; this time a polarization of students into conformers or radicals. The conformers—those who did not object to the fact that their schools and their school careers were being shaped to serve the national purpose—the schools rewarded. The radicals—those who rebelled—were not rewarded, and usually ended up ignored, or expelled by the system.

It was clear that the American faith in the power of the school had not been misplaced. The schools had indeed wrought a powerful influence. The schools had served the white middle-class suburbanites well, and they in turn hoped to secure future educational benevolence for their children. This smug satisfaction of those who had the greatest amount of control over its educational institutions gave little hope that America would see that its schools were an imperfect panacea.

EPILOGUE: A DECADE OF CRISIS

I

I now think that the theory of *The Imperfect Panacea* needs modification. At least in part. I argued that history did not uphold Americans' faith in the power of the schools to solve all social problems. I tried to show that the schools never did eliminate the evils nor cure the ills that had emerged in America in the second half of the nineteenth century. Indeed, I maintained that in trying to cope with the serious problems brought about by urbanization, industrialization, emancipation, and nationalization, the schools often exacerbated them.

I think this part of my thesis still holds—the part that says the schools have been an imperfect panacea. For in spite of all their efforts, the schools have not eliminated racism, nor secured equality of economic opportunity, nor created real urban communities, nor overcome widespread political powerlessness. And since the book first appeared we have witnessed how recent developments in the schools have made matters worse: forced busing has heightened racial tensions; decentralization and community control have sharpened community conflict and further eroded the basis of community; increased opportunity for schooling has diminished equality of economic opportunity by raising still higher the barrier of job credentials (as well as producing, of late, graduates with credentials for jobs that do not exist); increased involvement of the federal government in educational financing, programing, and research has heightened feelings of political powerlessness—many now see themselves, and others, manipulated, exploited, ripped off, and victimized by the giant leviathan.

I remain convinced that the schools cannot solve society's problems, but my critics have changed my mind about other parts of my original thesis. Initially the reactions of readers bewildered me. They seemed contradictory. On the one hand, people would assert that Americans had never really had the kind of faith I had attributed to them. Maybe educators had this faith, the argument went, and perhaps some philanthropists, and journalists, and even the political leaders I mention in the book—but by and large, my critics insisted, the American public does not now, and never did, regard the school as the panacea for social problems. (Some of my own students gently suggested I change the subtitle of the book to read: *American* Educators' *Faith in Education, 1865–1965.*)

On the other hand, critics (often the same ones!) would cite case after case of instances where the school had helped people overcome their *own* problems—of poverty, of discrimination, of powerlessness. Without the help of the schools, this argument went, no blacks, few poor, and hardly any immigrants could have risen in American society.

After a long time and numerous exchanges with my critics, I have concluded both critcisms are correct. Even though most American educators have viewed the school as society's problem solver, most other Americans have not, and do not. However, most Americans have viewed the school as the agency to help them or their children avoid or escape the social ills that might plague them. Many who have suffered, or who now suffer—from poverty, from poor housing, from feelings of powerlessness, or from simply being black—have looked to the school as a way of escaping or overcoming these problems. And those who have escaped often credit their schooling; they view the schools as their own personal panaceas.

Helping some people to escape from evils that afflict them does not eliminate those evils from society; we still have racial discrimination, poverty, ghettos, and widespread political powerlessness. The schools have not solved or eliminated society's problems; they have merely helped some people avoid or escape them. Or have they?

The events of the past decade raise serious questions about this supposed role of the schools. Have they helped people escape from society's ills? Can they? Should they? And the very fact that such questions have arisen makes clear the present uncertainty about the belief that the school can be a personal panacea—a belief unaffected by the first edition of this book.

II

Most educators have continued to believe that schools are supposed to solve all social problems. Their belief that the school is society's panacea makes them ready to construe any and all social problems as educational problems. Their renders them vulnerable to demands from special interest groups. The expanded demands on the schools from such groups in recent years inevitably undermined their authority and prestige, just as expanded demands on the government have undermined its authority and prestige. Schools simply cannot pull off all they are asked to do.

Of late, groups worried about pollution demanded that schools provide environmental education; those fearing overpopulation secured courses in sex education; and drug education programs emerged to combat the drug problem. Of course, these educational endeavors have not solved the problems. But more disturbing to many laymen is that these new educational programs are wasteful, not so much of money (although *that*, too), but of teachers' and students' time. Instead of teaching and learning those standard school subjects that help kids "get ahead," the schools waste time on these peripheral matters. Thus, the "idealism" of the educators who believe that the function of the school is to help solve society's problems collides with the parents' "selfish" belief that schools are supposed to help kids "make it," help them escape, or avoid, concrete ills like poverty, discrimination, and powerlessness.

This confrontation elicits from educators the response that they cannot be effective educators because they are beseiged by too many different demands. As I write I have before me a recent widely syndicated column by the conservative writer, James J. Kilpatrick. In an earlier column he blamed the teachers for the recently discovered continuous drop in scores on standard high school achievement tests. Here he now reports some of the explanations the teachers sent to him. All are variations on the now classic response: the days are not long enough for teachers to fulfill all the different responsibilities society has heaped upon them.

Converting social problems into educational problems and then turning them over to the school is a way for the adult world to avoid facing up to these problems (and, at the same time, a way to create a handy scapegoat—educators—when these problems fail to go away). But in recent years, when educators have announced that social problems were too much to handle, their adament and sophisticated critics construed such declarations as alibis to cover ineptitude and irresponsibility. These critics have generated and supported an increasingly powerful movement to secure accountability in the schools.

This confrontation between educators and their critics over matters of responsibility and accountability must be seen in the context of the movement toward unionization in the 1960's and 1970's as besieged teachers united to protect themselves and their jobs against the demands of special interest groups and budget cutters spurred on by an inflationary economy. Relations between the educators and their critics have become more acerbic as the critics accuse unionized teachers of selfish acts that belie any so-called idealism. The irony here is that it is the very idealism of the educators—the belief that schools can solve all of society's problems—that provoked the events that led to their present diminished authority and reduced prestige.

Even more ironic: at the very moment that teachers were accused of failing to help children escape the ills of society, other critics were revealing the empirical, logical, and moral contradictions inherent in this very belief that schools can or should do this. The growing awareness of these contradictions has deepened the uncertainty about what schools are for.

III

The initial attack on the belief that schools can help people escape the ills of society came with the publication in 1966 of the "Coleman Report," officially entitled: "Equality of Educational Opportunity, Report of the Office of Education to the Congress and the President" (U. S. Printing Office, July 1966). The Civil Rights Act of 1964 had required that the Commissioner of Education carry out a survey on the matter of equality of opportunity. As supervisor of that survey, James Coleman reported that black children suffered from inequality of opportunity. He concluded this after trying to assess how the differing distribution of resources affected children's achievement in schools attended by blacks, and in schools attended by whites. Coleman found that a significant gap in the achievement scores between black and white children was already present in the first grade—a gap that widened by the end of elementary school. Yet, somewhat surprisingly, Coleman found that there was little difference between white and black schools in such things as physical facilities, formal curricula, and other measurable criteria. For Coleman the interpretation was clear: Family background differences account for much more variation in achievement than do school deficiencies.

If the schools were not working, and—as presently constituted—could not work, for disadvantaged kids who attended all black schools, what could be done? Coleman found that children from disadvantaged backgrounds did somewhat better in schools that were predominantly middle class than in schools that were homogeneously lower class. The only hope for these kids, then, was to get them going to school with children from better educated backgrounds.

The Coleman Report became the basis for claims that the schools did not provide equality of opportunity. Subsequent abortive attempts to make them provide such equality led many blacks to conclude that this was conscious and deliberate—this is what schools were for: to hold black kids down. In city after city efforts to create equal opportunity for disadvantaged black children by sending (often busing) them to schools with middle-class white children met powerful, sometimes violent, resistance. Many blacks concluded that their schools were not escape hatches, but jails deliberately constructed to constrain their children to lives of discrimination and deprivation.

Not all behavioral scientists accepted Coleman's interpretation that the early differences in achievement scores between black and white children were due to family background. Arthur Jensen, for example, argued that 80 percent of a person's I.Q. is inherited, while environmental factors account for only 20 percent. Blacks, Jensen seemed to be saying, are innately inferior to whites as based on the measurements of I.Q. tests.

Richard Hernstein, another psychologist, combined the findings of Coleman and Jensen to argue that if the environment is equalized (Coleman's findings) and differences in mental abilities are inherited (Jensen's findings), then social standing itself will be based to some extent on inherited differences. Hernstein seemed to be arguing that in a society that provided equality of opportunity, blacks were, or would be, at the bottom—appropriately.

This emergence of the long-considered mythical notion of innate racial inferiority shocked and dismayed most educators and infuriated all black people. The upshot was a further undermining of commitment to the ideal of equality of opportunity, and with it a growing erosion of belief in the possibility of creating a truly meritocratic society. What many now rejected was the scientific methodology that purportedly assessed a person's true merit so as to guarantee equality of opportunity. "Is it possible," they asked, "to ascertain an individual's merit?" (How can we exactly measure what is due to genetic inheritances and what due to environment?) "Moreover, do tests of merit (e.g., I.Q. tests) measure true merit, or simply acquired skills?" Finally, "Is not every test of merit 'culture biased'? Hence, invalid?"

The Coleman Report appeared initially to be simply another complaint that the schools did not provide equality of opportunity for all, but it soon was interpreted as a declaration that the schools could *not* provide equality of opportunity for blacks. Explanations of why the schools could not provide this equality struck at the very foundation of the belief that schools can help people escape from the social ills that afflict them. Schools, many concluded, could not help blacks escape the evil of social discrimination because the very notion of equality of opportunity for all that was based solely upon merit was a myth—a myth, it was said, that was foisted on black victims to hold them down.

The second attack on the belief that the schools can help

people escape the ills of society was the so-called "Jencks Report of 1972," *Inequality: A Reassessment of the Effect of Family and Schooling in America.* Here the focus was on the economic results of schooling. In analyzing the Coleman data Jencks had found that students who scored high in achievement tests "were often enrolled in the same schools as the students who performed worst." In *Inequality* he maintains, "There is nearly as much economic inequality among brothers raised in the same house as in the general population. This means that inequality is recreated in each generation, even among people who start life in essentially identical circumstances." "Economic success," Jencks concludes, "seems to depend on varieties of luck and on-the-job competence that are only moderately related to family background, schooling, or scores in standardized tests."

Jencks and his associates presented reams of data and a highly involved argument to demonstrate that the schools could not help poor people escape from poverty. Such merit as the school might discover or foster in pupils is simply irrelevant to escaping from poverty, they argued, since economic success is largely a matter of luck. The only way to help people escape from poverty, Jencks says, is to eliminate economic inequality in the society, "creating what other countries usually call socialism." The creation of such a society, Jencks concludes, is not a task for the schools. Schools are marginal institutions in "dealing with such social, political, economic problems."

Up until this point many Americans had tolerated the existence of poverty and had accepted the society that permitted it to exist only because of the belief that schools *could* help people escape. By demonstrating the irrelevance of the school and its marginality to any real escape effort, the Jencks Report undermined commitment to the existing society.

While the work of social scientists weakened the faith of many in our present arrangements by demonstrating that the schools could not help the blacks or the poor, another attack was bursting forth from an unexpected quarter: from those who had already escaped, from those who had made it. It was the children who usually raised the doubts about the worth of the existing society. Many children of the affluent now seemed to reject the very prizes their parents had sought and won, wealth, power, security. During the late 1960's the doubters and the scoffers among the young became a full fledged "youth movement"—a movement in reaction against much that the older generation believed in or at least tacitly accepted. The young who identified with the movement were anti-war, anti-middle class, anti-technology, anti-capitalism, anti-schools-that-processed-people-into-personnel, and anti-education-based-on-competition. Many of the young questioned the value of an education that merely led to living-in-a-big-house-in-the-suburbs. They did not look to the schools as an agency to help them move up in the society; they did not see schools as an escape route to some higher level of the society. Many, instead, wanted to create a new society, a new culture, a counter-culture—a society, a culture, a civilization where people could peacefully and more equitably share the goods of the earth.

On moral grounds, then, the youth movement rejected the very idea of a meritocratic society and the educational system that was supposed to sustain it. A meritocratic society and meritocratic schools, they claimed, simply generate selfish competition to possess prizes and foster undesirable human habits—pride, gluttony, greed, envy, sloth, covetousness, anger.

A part of the youth movement, but at the same time an independent development, was the reaction of many of the young to the Vietnam War. Those who most opposed U. S. involvement in the war were college students using the educational system to postpone or escape military conscription. Frequently their rage against the war exploded in protest against colleges and universities that collaborated with the government in pursuit of war policies—collaborated through research, through officer training programs, through providing military deferments for the "less expendable" youths.

Their reaction against the conduct of this war led many young people to question the value of going to school in order to secure power and influence in the society. As they now saw it, schooling too often transformed people into manipulators and exploiters. Degrees and diplomas were tickets of entry into the corrupt power structure of society. So here, too, we witness a rejection on moral grounds of a meritocratic society and meritocratic schools. As these critics saw it, schools could help people overcome their powerlessness, but at a terrific moral cost. Better then, they concluded, not to enter the corridors of power, the realms of the ruling elite. And better change the functions of the schools, too.

IV

Much of the educational history written during this decade reflected these attacks on established educational institutions. The same empirical, logical, and moral arguments were marched forth to demonstrate that American schools had never really helped people escape the ills of society. These revisionist historians set out to shatter the illusions and destroy the myths about our schools. Michael Katz, for example, in *Class, Bureaucracy, and Schools* argued that as far back as the nineteenth century, American schools had discriminated against various ethnic and racial groups and had exhibited a strong bias against the poor. Histories of the testing movement, written by Joel Spring and by Clarence Karier, revealed the longstanding logical inadequacies of the efforts to assess true merit. Colin Greer in *The Great School Legend* laid bare the moral hypocrisy of a meritocratic educational system that continually fails 40 percent if its students, a task Greer suggests schools were deliberately set up to carry out.

This revisionist history darkened and deepened the crisis of faith in American education. Until this point the arguments had been about facts and the interpretation of facts:

Were the schools helping people? Were they helping the poor? the blacks? the powerless? Were the schools doing all they could? These arguments had taken place within a consensual framework. Everyone was committed to the notion that schools were supposed to help people, and believed that everyone else felt the same way, too; this is what schools were supposed to be for.

The revisionist historians shattered this consensus and polarized the discussants into good guys and bad guys—the persecutors and their victims. The schools, according to these revisionists, had never helped the poor, the blacks, the powerless—not because this was difficult to do and educators are fallible, but because the real purpose of the school (the hidden purpose) was to hold people down. The notion that schools in the past had helped people escape was, they insisted, simply a myth—a myth long used to conceal the actual reactionary purpose of schooling.

In place of the consensual framework there now emerged a disjunctive outlook that insisted one was either part of the problem or part of the solution. And schools, these historians had made clear, were not part of the solution.

These broadsides against schools and educators further subverted their prestige and authority. Educators, most of whom considered themselves idealists and members of an idealistic profession, now found segments of the public arrayed against them because they were the enemy, the destroyers of the dream of progress and improvement. Thus many of the educational policies enacted or proposed during this period were directed at reducing or proscribing the authority of professional educators; decentralization, community control, the abolition of compulsory education are some examples. One notes that Michael Katz endorsed all these in his book on the history of bureaucracy in the schools. In addition, he suggested that we further reduce the prestige and authority of teachers by restricting them solely to the teaching of skills.

v

If schools were not working to help people escape the ills of society—something, according to the revisionist historians, they had never done—then what was to be done? Many called for radical changes in the educational enterprise. For the first time in our educational history, radical proposals for educational change received serious and widespread attention. Bestselling books, articles in scholarly journals and popular magazines, television shows, lecture tours, and college classrooms all served as vehicles to promote the proposals for radical change—and to promote the names of the radical critics who proposed them.

The proposals for radical reform came in three waves, each succeeding wave signaling deeper disillusion with existing educational arrangements.

The initial band of radical critics simply sought to eliminate those features of the established educational system that prevented the schools from helping people. John Holt denounced the prescribed curriculum; Neil Postman and Charles Weingartner ridiculed the passive, subject-centered methods teachers used; Herbert Kohl and Jonathan Kozol excoriated the customary unfriendly, depersonalized, even lethal, atmosphere and ambiance in most classrooms and schools.

In time some of these critics saw the inadequacy of their own radical proposals. A smorgasbord curriculum, or an inquiry method of teaching, or open classrooms, just did not go far enough. Some, like Kohl and Kozol, joined others, like Dennison, Rossman, and Graubard, who argued that it was not possible to reform the existing schools. The established schools reflect the existing society, their argument went, so to change the schools one must first change the society. And to change the society one had to create new, different schools —free schools. Such schools would be free from the constraints society had imposed on them in order to preserve the status quo.

Finally, some critics announced that free or alternate schools were not enough, either. A more radical revolution was needed. So John Holt and others joined with Ivan Illich and Everett Reimer in pronouncing that reformed schools, even radically reformed schools, were not the solution; schools were the *problem*. We must de-school society, they said; expunge the school from society. Only then will a different, better, civilization emerge—a peaceful, egalitarian, sharing civilization.

With this last wave of radical critics we reach the edge of educational nihilism. At this juncture many educators got off the bandwagon of radical educational reform.

Those educators most influenced by the radical critics continued to maintain that the school's efforts to help people overcome the social ills that plagued them were both futile and misguided. Many turned away from the social, the political, and the economic functions of the school to zero in more on the personal and individual benefits of schooling. They stress the affective development of students and call themselves humanistic educators. Following the lead of the founders of humanistic psychology, Abraham Maslow and Carl Rogers, and sometimes of neo-Freudians like A. S. Neil, or even the more esoteric transpersonal psychologists, these humanistic educators construe the schools as places where students realize their human potential.

Yet, many educators today seem untouched by the radical criticism of the past decade. Much is afoot that excites their enthusiasm and interest: individualized instruction, competency-based teaching, open classrooms, career education. None of these educational strategies are new. More important is that in an almost mindless way they reflect a continuing faith in the efforts of the school to help those who "deserve it" (the meritorious) to "make it" and thereby escape poverty, powerlessness, and discrimination. It seems as if most educators have backed away from the fundamental questions raised over the past decade. What are schools for? What are teachers for? What's worth knowing? Having seemingly weathered the crisis of faith, most are back to the routine of maintaining the existing arrangements. The rituals of schooling fortify them, as does their conviction that their motives are pure.

Yet, the questions remain. If our schools are not a panacea —if they cannot solve the problems of society, *nor help people escape from those problems*—then what are schools for? What are teachers for? What's worth knowing?

BIBLIOGRAPHIC NOTE

ONE: THE AMERICANS AND THEIR SCHOOLS

In this rapid survey of the pre-Civil War functions of the American school I have drawn freely on the work of Daniel Boorstin, *The Americans, The Colonial Experience* (New York: Random House, 1958), Rush Welter, *Popular Education and Democratic Thought in America* (New York: Columbia University Press, 1962), and Bernard Bailyn, *Education in the Forming of American Society* (Chapel Hill: University of North Carolina Press, 1960). I have also used the interpretations of the role of higher education given by Frederick Rudolph, *The American College and University* (New York: Alfred A. Knopf, 1962) and Richard Hofstadter and Walter P. Metzger, *The Development of Academic Freedom in the United States* (New York: Columbia University Press, 1955).

TWO: RACIAL INEQUALITY AND THE SCHOOLS

My account of the Yankee teachers in the South is based on the work of Henry Lee Swint, *The Northern Teacher in the South* (Nashville: Vanderbilt University Press, 1941). The attempt of the Southern states to set up a system of education is treated by Edgar W. Knight in *Public Education in the South* (Boston: Ginn, 1922) and Charles W. Dabney, *Universal Education in the South* (Chapel Hill: University of North Carolina Press, 1932). For the battle against the Freedmen's Bureau, I have relied upon John Hope Franklin's *Reconstruction: After the Civil War* (Chicago: University of Chicago Press, 1961). I have leaned heavily on this work as well as his monumental, *From Slavery to Freedom* (New York: Alfred A. Knopf, 1937). Much of my discussion of this period was also influenced by C. Vann Woodward's *Origins of the New South 1877–1913* (Baton Rouge: Louisiana State University Press, 1951). I have also consulted Walter L. Fleming's *Documentary History of Reconstruction* (New York: Peter Smith, 1950). Chapter IX of the second volume contains documents pertaining to "Educational Problems of Reconstruction."

I have based most of my discussion of the Peabody Fund on the history written by J. L. M. Curry, *A Brief Sketch of George Peabody, and a History of the Peabody Education Fund* (Cambridge: J. Wilson & Son, 1898). An excellent recent study is Earle H. West, "The Peabody Education Fund and Negro Education," *History of Education Quarterly*, vol. VI, no. 2 (Summer 1966).

The picture of Negro education during the eighties and nineties is based on Woodward (*op. cit.*) and Horace Mann Bond, *The Education of the Negro in the American Social Order* (New York: Prentice-Hall, 1934). C. Vann Woodward's *The Strange Career of Jim Crow* (New York: Oxford University Press, 1957) supplied the data for my discussion of the Populist movement in the South.

For the career of Booker T. Washington I used his autobiography, *Up from Slavery* (New York: Doubleday, Page, 1901). I quoted from this and also from his *Selected Speeches* (Garden City: Doubleday, 1932). I also found Rayford W. Logan, *The Negro in American Life and Thought: The Nadir, 1877–1890* (New York: Dial, 1954) helpful. For the career of William E. B. Du Bois I used the biography by Francis L. Broderick, *W. E. B. Du Bois: Negro Leader in Time of Crisis* (Stanford: Stanford University Press, 1959). The quote from Du Bois is from his *The Souls of Black Folks* (Chicago: A. C. McClurg, 1903).

My interpretation of recent developments has been influenced by Louis Lomax, *The Negro Revolt* (New York: Harper & Row, 1962), Howard Brotz, *The Black Jews of Harlem* (New York: Free Press, 1964), Charles E. Silberman, *Crisis in Black and White* (New York: Random House, 1964), and Nathan Glazer, "Negroes and Jews: The New Challenge to Pluralism," *Commentary*, vol. 38, no. VI (December 1964).

THREE: THE CITY AND THE SCHOOLS

For the growth of the city I have used Arthur M. Schlesinger, *The Rise of the City, 1878–1898* (New York: Macmillan, 1933), Blake McKelvey, *The Urbanization of America* (New Brunswick: Rutgers University Press, 1963), Constance McLaughlin Green, *The Rise of Urban America* (New York: Harper & Row, 1965), and Charles N. Glaab, *The American City, A Documentary History* (Homewood, Ill.: Dorsey Press, 1963), especially Chapter III. Maldwyn Jones, *American Immigration* (Chicago: University of Chicago Press, 1960) supplied much of the information on immigrants.

For my description of the impact of the city on the immigrant families I have relied on Oscar Handlin, *The Uprooted* (Boston: Little, Brown, 1951) and the essays in a volume he edited, *The Historian and the City* (Cambridge: M.I.T. Press, 1963). I have also been influenced by Mary Antin's *The Promised Land* (Boston: Houghton Mifflin, 1912).

The reaction to the immigrants is best described in the works of Jacob Riis. I consulted *How the Other Half Lives* (New York: Scribner's, 1903) and *The Battle with the Slums* (New York: Macmillan, 1902). The Americanization movement is treated in Edward G. Hartmann, *The Movement to Americanize the Immigrant* (New York: Columbia University Press, 1948), and John Higham, *Strangers in the Land: Patterns of American Nativism 1860–1925* (New Brunswick: Rutgers University Press, 1955).

The data on compulsory education was obtained from Forest C. Ensign, *Compulsory School Attendance and Child Labor* (Iowa City: Athens Press, 1921) and John L. Lawing, *Standards for State and Local Compulsory School Attendance Service* (Maryville, Mo.: Forum Print Shop, 1934).

A good summary of the growth of the educational enterprise during this period can be found in Ernest Carroll Moore, *Fifty Years of American Education: A Sketch of the Progress of Education in the United States for 1867–1917* (Boston: Ginn, 1917). More detailed information is found in Nicholas M. Butler, ed., *Education in the United States* (New York: American Book Company, 1910), Douglas E. Lawson, *Curriculum Development in City School Systems* (Chicago: University of Chicago Press, 1940), and Arthur Henry Chamberlain, *The Growth of Responsibility and Enlargement of Power of the City School Superintendent* (Berkeley: University of California Press, 1913). The sorry plight of the urban schools of the period is depicted in Joseph Mayer Rice's *The Public School System of the United States* (New York: The Century Company, 1893) and a brief introduction to the beginnings of school administration is Elwood P. Cubberly, *Public School Administration* (Boston: Houghton Mifflin, 1916).

William T. Harris lavished praise on the graded school

in numerous writings. I quoted from one of them, "Elementary Education," in *Monographs on Education in the United States*, No. 3 (Albany: J. B. Lyon Company, 1904). I found some helpful material on specialization in W. S. Deffenbaugh, "Public Education in the Cities of the U.S.," U.S. Bureau of Education, Bulletin 1918, No. 48 (Washington, D.C.: Government Printing Office, 1919).

John D. Philbrick describes the new city normal schools in *City School Systems in the United States* (Washington, D.C.: Government Printing Office, 1885). The work of Edward Sheldon at Oswego is discussed by Andrew P. Hollis, *The Contributions of the Oswego Normal School to Educational Progress in the United States* (Boston: Heath, 1898). I found the quote from Elizabeth Mayo's *Manual* in Lois C. Mossman's *Changing Conceptions Relative to the Planning of Lessons* (New York: Teachers College, Columbia University, 1924).

The study of dropouts in St. Louis appeared in the U.S. Commissioner of Education Report for 1899–1900. For the Herbartians I found helpful Charles De Garmo's *Herbart and the Herbartians* (New York: Scribner's Sons, 1895). The *Yearbooks* of the National Herbart Society for the Scientific Study of Teaching were published from 1895 to 1898. Its successor, the National Society for the Scientific Study of Education (later, the National Society for the Study of Education) began to publish yearbooks in 1901.

I based my description of John Dewey's Laboratory School on the account in Katherine Camp Mayhew and Anna Camp Edwards, *The Dewey School* (New York: Appleton-Century, 1936). The quote from Edward Ward about social centers appears in Clarence A. Perry, *Wider Use of the School Plant* (New York: Charities Publication Committee, Russell Sage Foundation, 1910). The quote from Lord Bryce is from *Modern Democracies* (New York: Macmillan, 1921). The description of the "community school" of the thirties is based on the volume edited by Samuel Everett, *The Community School* (New York: Appleton-Century,

1938). The quotes from Arthur Bestor are from his *Educational Wastelands* (Urbana, Ill.: University of Illinois Press, 1953). The quote from Richard Hofstadter about intellectuals in the 1950's is from his *Anti-Intellectualism in American Life* (New York: Alfred A. Knopf, 1963). I obtained the statistics for the fifties and sixties from Oscar Handlin's *The Newcomers* (Cambridge: Harvard University Press, 1954) and from the collection of articles in *The Schools and the Urban Crisis*, edited by August Kerker and Barbara Bonmarito (New York: Holt, Rinehart and Winston, 1965); the quote from James B. Conant is also in this volume. Most of the material on the urban Negro is from Charles E. Silberman, *Crisis in Black and White* (New York: Random House, 1964).

FOUR: ECONOMIC OPPORTUNITY AND THE SCHOOLS

For the history of the labor movement I used John R. Commons (*et al.*), *History of Labor in the United States* (New York: Macmillan, 1926), Henry Pelling, *American Labor* (Chicago: University of Chicago Press, 1961), and Philip S. Foner, *History of the Labor Movement in the United States* (New York: International Publishers, 1955).

The material on the American businessmen is based on Sigmund Diamond, *The Reputation of American Businessmen* (Cambridge: Harvard University Press, 1955), Matthew Josephson, *The Robber Barons* (New York: Harcourt, Brace, 1934), Stewart H. Holbrook, *The Age of the Moguls* (New York: Doubleday, 1953), and Edward C. Kirkland, *Dream and Thought in the Business Community 1860–1900* (Chicago: Quadrangle Books, 1964).

Most of what I say about the American success literature is based on Irwin G. Wyllie, *The Self-Made Man in America* (New Brunswick: Rutgers University Press, 1954). I also used Robert D. Mosier, *Making the American Mind* (New York: King's Crown Press, 1941) for this genre of literature as well as for his analysis of the *McGuffey's*

Readers. Louis B. Wright, "Franklin's Legacy to the Gilded Age," *Virginia Quarterly Review,* vol. XXII, no. 2 (Spring 1946), was useful. I also found helpful Charles Carpenter, *History of American Schoolbooks* (Philadelphia: University of Pennsylvania Press, 1963). John Tebbel has a brief, informative study of Horatio Alger, *From Rags to Riches* (New York: Macmillan, 1963). I also found helpful John Cawelti, *Apostles of the Self-Made Man* (Chicago: University of Chicago Press, 1965).

William Miller's analyses of the business elite appear in a book he edited, *Men in Business* (New York: Harper Torchbooks, 1962) and in an essay in *The Reconstruction of American History* (New York: Harper Torchbooks, 1963), edited by John Higham. The disenchantment of Americans during the eighties is sketched briefly in Samuel P. Hays, *The Response to Industrialism* (Chicago: University of Chicago Press, 1957) and Eric Goldman, *Rendezvous with Destiny* (New York: Alfred A. Knopf, 1952) and more fully in Chester A. Destler, *American Radicalism* (New London: Octagon, 1946). For the commentary of one who personally experienced that disenchantment, see Richard T. Ely, *Social Aspects of Christianity* (New York: T. Y. Crowell & Company, 1889). In addition to Andrew Carnegie's *Triumphant Democracy* (New York: Scribner's, 1886), I have quoted from two collections of his essays: *Empire of Business* (New York: Doubleday, Page, 1902) and the *Gospel of Wealth and Other Timely Essays,* edited by Edward C. Kirkland (Cambridge: Belknap Press of Harvard University, 1962). For what I say about Carnegie I am indebted to Robert G. McCloskey, *American Conservatism in the Age of Enterprise* (New York: Harper Torchbooks, 1964). The *Report* of the Mosely Education Commission was published by the Commission in London, 1904.

For the development of vocationalism in higher education I am heavily indebted to the brilliant study by Laurence R. Veysey, *The Emergence of the American University* (Chicago: University of Chicago Press, 1965) and to Frederick

Rudolph, *American College and University* (New York: Alfred A. Knopf, 1962).

I. L. Kandel's statistics for the number of high schools in 1860 appear in his *History of Secondary Education* (Boston: Houghton Mifflin, 1930). The comparative study of high school programs in the nineteenth century is John E. Stout's famous *The Development of High School Curricula in the North Central States from 1860 to 1918* (Chicago: University of Chicago Press, 1921).

In discussing the work of the Committee of Ten, I have profited greatly from Theodore Sizer, *Secondary Schools at the Turn of the Century* (New Haven: Yale University Press, 1964) and from Edward Krug, *The Shaping of the American High School* (New York: Harper & Row, 1964). I also used the study of the Carnegie Unit made by E. Tompkins and W. Gaumnitz, published as "The Carnegie Unit: Its Origin, Status and Trends" (United States Department of Health, Education and Welfare Bulletin No. 7, 1954).

For the beginnings of vocational education in the schools, I used Charles A. Bennett, *History of Manual and Industrial Education 1870 to 1917* (Peoria, Ill.: Manual Arts Press, 1937), Grant Venn, *Man, Education and Work* (Washington, D.C., American Council on Education, 1964), and Edward Krug (*op. cit.*). *The Report of the Massachusetts Commission on Industrial and Technical Education* (The Douglas Commission) was published by the Commission in Boston in 1906. The proceedings of the meetings of the National Society for the Promotion of Industrial Education were published in New York by the Society as *Bulletins*, beginning in 1907. All talks delivered at NEA conventions are published yearly by the association as *Proceedings*.

The report of the Commission on the Reorganization of Secondary Schools was published as a Bulletin (No. 35) of the Bureau of Education as "Cardinal Principles of Secondary Education" (Washington, D.C.: Government Printing Office, 1918).

The studies by Robert and Helen Lynd are *Middletown* (New York: Harcourt, Brace, 1929), and *Middletown in Transition* (New York: Harcourt, Brace, 1937). The study conducted by Warner, Havinghurst, and Loeb is *Who Shall Be Educated?* (New York: Harper, 1944). The book I refer to by Patricia C. Sexton is *Education and Income* (New York: Viking, 1961).

The term "The Expert Society" is taken from the valuable book by Burton R. Clark, *Educating the Expert Society* (San Francisco: Chandler, 1962). I also used *Education and Manpower* (New York: Columbia University Press, 1960), edited by Henry David.

The essay by David Bazelon is "The New Class," *Commentary*, vol. 42, no. II (August 1966). Paul Goodman uses the phrase "The Universal Trap" in *Compulsory Mis-Education* (New York: Horizon, 1964).

FIVE: THE GOVERNMENT AND THE SCHOOLS

For information about the political situation after the Civil War, I used Thomas C. Cochran and William Miller, *The Age of Enterprise* (New York: Harper & Row, 1961; revised edition), Richard Hofstadter, *The American Political Tradition* (New York: Alfred A. Knopf, 1948), Samuel P. Hays, *The Response to Industrialism* (Chicago: University of Chicago Press, 1957), and Eric Goldman, *Rendezvous with Destiny* (New York: Vintage Books, 1956; revised edition).

My interpretation of the response of the liberal reformers leans heavily on Rush Welter, *Popular Education and Democratic Thought in America* (New York: Columbia University Press, 1962). I also found Goldman (*op. cit.*) helpful.

For the work and thought of William T. Harris I found invaluable Merle Curti, *The Social Ideas of American Educators* (Paterson, N.J.: Littlefield, Adams, 1963; revised edition) and Lawrence A. Cremin, *The Transformation of the School* (New York: Alfred A. Knopf, 1961). I also consulted John R. Anscott, "Moral Freedom and the Educative Process, A Study in the Educational Philosophy of William Torrey Harris" (Unpublished Ph.D. dissertation, New York University, 1948), John S. Roberts, *William T. Harris, A Critical Study of his Educational and Related Philosophical Views* (Washington, D.C.: National Education Association, 1924), and *William Torrey Harris, 1835–1935,* edited by Edward L. Schaub (Chicago: Open Court, 1936).

For my discussion on Charles W. Eliot I used the work of Frederick Rudolph, *The American College and University* (New York: Alfred A. Knopf, 1962), Laurence R. Veysey, *The Emergence of the American University* (Chicago: University of Chicago Press, 1965), and above all Samuel Eliot Morrison, *Three Centuries of Harvard* (Cambridge: Harvard University Press, 1936). I made extensive use of Eliot's essays collected in *American Contributions to Civilization* (New York: Century, 1898) and those collected and edited by Edward Krug, *Charles W. Eliot and Popular Education* (New York: Teachers College, Columbia University, 1961).

In my treatment of progressive politics I used all the works cited earlier (in the first two paragraphs) plus Richard Hofstadter, *The Age of Reform* (New York: Alfred A. Knopf, 1955). (Recently, in "Woodrow Wilson's Prediction to Frank Cobb: Words Historians Should Doubt Ever Got Spoken," *The Journal of American History,* vol. LVI, no. 3 (December 1967), Jerold S. Auerbach raised considerable doubt concerning the authenticity of the oft-quoted remarks Woodrow Wilson supposedly made to Frank Cobb.)

For my remarks on G. Stanley Hall and Edward Lee Thorndike I made use of *Psychology and the Science of Education,* edited by Geraldine M. Joncich (New York: Teachers College, Columbia University, 1962) and *Health, Growth, and Heredity,* edited by Charles E. Strickland and Charl‹ Burgess (New York: Teachers College, Columbia University, 1965). I also found Cremin (*op. cit.*) helpful.

My discussion of John Dewey is based on my reading of his *Reconstruction in Philosophy* (Boston: Beacon, 1948),

The Quest for Certainty (New York: Minton, Balch, 1929), *The School and Society* (Chicago: University of Chicago Press, 1943), *Democracy and Education* (New York: Macmillan, 1916), *How We Think* (New York: Henry Holt, 1922), and *Experience and Education* (New York: Macmillan, 1938).

My remarks on the University of Wisconsin were based, in part, on Frederick C. Howe, *Wisconsin: An Experiment in Democracy* (New York: Scribner's, 1912), Merle Curti and Vernon Curstensen, *The University of Wisconsin: A History*, Volume II (Madison: University of Wisconsin Press, 1949), and Charles McCarthy, *The Wisconsin Idea* (New York: Macmillan, 1912).

For the description of the post-progressive period I used Hofstadter, *The Age of Reform*, Goldman (*op. cit.*), and Arthur M. Schlesinger, Jr., *The Crisis of the Old Order* (Boston: Houghton Mifflin, 1957). I also found helpful John Chamberlain's *Farewell to Reform* (New York: Liveright, 1932).

In addition to Harold O. Rugg and Ann Shumaker's *The Child-Centered School* (Yonkers: World Book, 1928), I used Rugg's *Foundations for American Education* (Yonkers: World Book, 1947).

The section on the New Deal rests heavily on the interpretation of Richard Hofstadter. I also found helpful Sidney Fine, *Laissez Faire and the General-Welfare State* (Ann Arbor: University of Michigan Press, 1956).

For the work of the American Youth Commission I consulted *Youth and the Future* (Washington, D.C.: American Council on Education, 1942), and Homer P. Rainey, *How Fare American Youth?* (New York: Appleton-Century, 1938).

For my discussion of the group at Teachers College I used Cremin (*op. cit.*). *The Educational Frontier*, edited by William H. Kilpatrick (New York: The Century Co., 1933), was also published as *Yearbook XXI* of the National Society of College Teachers of Education. *Reorganizing*

Secondary Education (New York: Appleton-Century, 1939) was prepared by V. T. Thayer, Caroline B. Zachary and Ruth Kotinsky for the Commission on Secondary School Curriculum. K. L. Heaton and G. R. Koopman authored *A College Curriculum Based on Functional Needs of Students* (Chicago: University of Chicago Press, 1936). I profited from Thayer's description of the whole period in *Formative Ideas in American Education* (New York: Dodd, Mead, 1965). John F. Latimer's book is *What's Happened to Our High Schools?* (Washington, D.C.: Public Affairs Press, 1938). B. Paul Komisar's " 'Need' and the Needs-Curriculum" is in B. O. Smith and R. H. Emnis, *Language and Concepts in Education* (Chicago: Rand McNally, 1961).

I found parts of Daniel Bell's *The Reforming of General Education* (New York: Columbia University Press, 1966) helpful for understanding what is happening today. I also found Cremin (*op. cit.*) of value here. The 1958 quote from the Chancellor of the University of Kansas came from *Federal Educational Policies, Programs and Proposals* (Washington, D.C.: U.S. Government Printing Office, 1960). Admiral Hyman Rickover's best seller was *Education and Freedom* (New York: Dutton, 1959).

In addition to Clark Kerr's *The Uses of the University* (New York: Harper Torchbooks, 1966), I profited from Hal Draper's essay, "The Mind of Clark Kerr" in *Revolution at Berkeley* (New York: Dell, 1965), edited by Michael V. Miller and Susan Gilmore.

EPILOGUE: A DECADE OF CRISIS

A great number of historical analyses of recent education have appeared since the first edition of *The Imperfect Panacea*. Here are some of the most noteworthy: Fred and Grace Hechinger, *Growing up in America* (New York: McGraw-Hill, 1975); Geraldine Joncich Clifford, *The Shape of American Education* (Englewood Cliffs, N.J.: Prentice-Hall,

1975) and Charles E. Silberman, *Crisis in the Classroom* (New York: Random House, 1970). A brief, sprightly, overview of some of the issues and many of the figures active during the last decade can be found in *The School Book* by Neil Postman and Charles Weingartner (New York: Delacorte, 1973).

Some recent histories of American education that include analyses of recent events are: Diane Ravitch, *The Great School War* (New York: Basic Books, 1974); David B. Tyack, *The One Best System,* (Cambridge Mass: Harvard University Press, 1974); Walter Feinberg, *Reason and Rhetoric: The Intellectual Foundations of 20th Century Liberal Educational Policy* (New York: John Wiley & Sons, 1975); Clarence J. Karier, *Shaping the American Educational State: 1900 to the Present* (New York: The Free Press, 1975); and Robert L. Church, *Education in the United States* (New York: The Free Press, 1976).

Responses to the Coleman Report (James S. Coleman, et. al., "Equality of Educational Opportunity, Report of the Office of Education to Congress and the President" [U.S. Printing Office, July 1966]) are contained in Frederick Mosteller and Daniel P. Moynihan, eds., *On Equality of Educational Opportunity* (New York: Random House, 1972) and in *The Harvard Educational Review* XXXVIII (Winter 1968).

A helpful bibliography is Francisco Cordasco, *The Equality of Educational Opportunity* (Totowa, N.J.: Littlefield, Adams and Co., 1973).

Responses to the "Jencks Report" (Christopher Jencks and Associates, *Inequality: A Reassessment of the Effects of Family and Schooling in America* [New York: Basic Books, 1972]) are in *The Harvard Educational Review* XLIII (February 1973). A study claiming to refute Jencks' findings was published by Herbert H. Hyman, Charles R. Wright, and John Shelton Reed called *The Enduring Effects of Education* (Chicago: The University of Chicago Press, 1975), but see also the critical review of this study by one of Jencks' asso-

250 | Bibliographic Note

ciates, Mary Jo Bane, in *The Review of Education* II (July–August 1976).

Responses to Arthur Jensen's controversial article ("How Much Can We Boost IQ and Scholastic Achievement?" *Harvard Educational Review* XXXIX (Winter 1969), appeared in *The Harvard Educational Review* XXXIX (Spring and Summer 1969). Richard Herrnstein's articles "IQ" appeared in *Atlantic Monthly* CCXXVIII (September 1971). Two collections of reading on the IQ controversy are: W. J. Bloch and Gerald Dworkin, *The IQ Controversy* (New York: Pantheon, 1975), and Alan Gartner, Colin Greer and Frank Riessman, *The New Assault on Equality: IQ and Social Stratification* (New York: Harper & Row, 1974).

Analyses and critiques of meritocracy and education appear in Daniel Bell, *The Coming of Post Industrial Society* (New York: Basic Books, 1973); Samuel Bowles and Herbert Gintis, *Schooling in Capitalist America* (New York: Basic Books, 1976); and Joel Spring, *The Sorting Machine: National Educational Policy Since 1945* (New York: David McKay, 1976).

The leading "revisionist" histories published during this period were those of Michael Katz, *The Irony of Early School Reform* (Cambridge: Harvard University Press, 1968); *Class, Bureaucracy, and Schools: The Illusion of Educational Change in America* (New York: Praeger Publishers, 1971) and Colin Greer, *The Great School Legend: A Revisionist Interpretation of American Public Education* (New York: Basic Books, 1972). A collection of "revisionist" essays edited by Clarence J. Karier, Paul Violas, and Joel Spring called *Roots of Crisis: American Education in the Twentieth Century* (Chicago: Rand McNally, 1973) contains Clarence Karier's critique of the testing movement. Joel Spring's critique is in Edgar B. Gumbert and Joel Spring, *The Superschool and the Superstate: American Education in the Twentieth Century* (New York: John Wiley and Sons, 1974).

The most important works of what I have called the initial band of romantic critics are: John Holt, *How Children Fail*

(New York: Pitman, 1967); Neil Postman and Charles Weingartner, *Teaching As a Subversive Activity* (New York: Delacorte, 1969); Herbert Kohl, *36 Children* (New York: New American Library, 1967); Jonathan Kozol, *Death at an Early Age: The Destruction of the Hearts and Minds of Negro Children in the Boston Public Schools* (Boston: Houghton Mifflin, 1967). Three books that chart the course of the free school movement are: George Dennison, *The Lives of Children* (New York: Random House, 1969); Jonathan Kozol, *Free Schools* (Boston: Houghton Mifflin, 1972); and Allen Graubard, *Free The Children: Radical Reform and the Free School Movement* (New York: Random House, 1973). The theories put forth in *Deschooling Society* (New York: Harper & Row, 1970) by Ivan Illich and in *School is Dead* (New York: Doubleday, 1971) by Everett Reimer are critically assessed in *After Deschooling, What?* (New York: Harper & Row, 1973), edited by Alan Gartner, Colin Greer, and Frank Riessman. Excerpts from many of the romantic educational critics are anthologized in *Radical School Reform* (New York: Simon and Schuster, 1969) edited by Ronald and Beatrice Gross; and in *Innovations in Education: Reformers and their Critics* (Boston: Allyn and Bacon, 1975), edited by John Martin Rich. There are critiques of the movement in *Radical School Reform: Critiques and Alternatives* (Boston: Little, Brown and Co., 1973), edited by Cornelius J. Troost; and in Henry J. Perkinson *Two Hundred Years of American Educational Thought* (New York: David McKay, 1976).

Two recently published and helpful guides to the history of American education are: Francisco Cordasco and William W. Brickman, *A Bibliography of American Educational History* (New York: AMS Press, 1975); and Sol Cohen's monumental *Education in the United States: A Documentary History* (New York: Random House, 1974, 5 volumes.)

INDEX

ABOUT THE AUTHOR

Henry J. Perkinson teaches at New York University. He has written *Two Hundred Years of American Education* (1976), *The Possibilities of Error: An Approach to Education* (1971) and co-edited *The Educational Man: Studies in the History of Educational Thought* (1965). He was editor of the *History of Education Quarterly* and now edits *The Review of Education*.